Air War over Syria
Su-24M

Russian Aerospace Group
September 2015 – March 2016

HUGH HARKINS

Copyright © 2017 Hugh Harkins

All rights reserved.

ISBN: 1903630665
ISBN-13: 978-1903630662

Air War over Syria
Su-24M

Russian Aerospace Group
September 2015-March 2016

© Hugh Harkins 2017

Published by Centurion Publishing
United Kingdom

ISBN 10: 1903630665
ISBN 13: 978-1903630662

This volume first published in 2017

The Author is identified as the copyright holder of this work under sections 77 and 78 of the Copyright Designs and Patents Act 1988

Cover design © Centurion Publishing & Createspace

Page layout, concept and design © Centurion Publishing

All rights reserved. No part of this publication may be reproduced, stored in a retrieval system, transmitted in any form, or by any means, electronic, mechanical or photocopied, recorded or otherwise, without the written permission of the Publisher

The Publisher and Author would like to thank all organisations for their assistance and contributions in the preparation of this volume: JSC Sukhoi; Novosibirsk Aircraft Plant, Chkalov; Komsomolsk-on-Amur Aircraft Production Association; UAC (United Aircraft Corporation); JSC Salut; JSC Tactical Missiles Corporation; JSC Concern Radio-Electronic Technologies (KRET); Rostec Corporation; JSC Electroavtomatica; Rosoboronexport; Armaco; US Department of Defense and the Ministry of Defence of the Russian Federation

CONTENTS

	INTRODUCTION	i
1	THE SYRIAN CIVIL WAR – RUSSIA INTERVENES	3
2	SUKHOI Su-24M STRIKE AIRCRAFT	7
3	THE RUSSIAN AIR CAMPAIGN – THE OPENING PHASE	35
4	SDA GROUND OFFENSIVES – OCTOBER 2015-MARCH 2016	57
5	CHRONOLOGY OF RUSSIAN AEROSPACE GROUP OPERATIONS IN SYRIA FROM 23 OCTOBER 2015-15 MARCH 2016, WITH SPECIFICS OF SLECTED Su-24M OPERATIONS	67
6	THE SHOOTDOWN OF WHITE 83	111
7	APPENDICES	121
8	GLOSSARY	122

INTRODUCTION

The primary remit of this volume is to document the bombing operations against Islamic State (Islamic State of Iraq and the Levant) and other opposition groups by the Sukhoi Su-24M strike aircraft detachment of the Russian Aerospace Group in the Syrian Arab Republic from 30 September 2015 through mid-March 2016.

While the volume is not intended to be a descriptive monograph for the Su-24 strike aircraft, a basic description of the genesis, development and fielding of the weapon system is provided, as are relevant chapters that focus on the initial combat operations phase of the Russian Aerospace Group, Syrian Democratic Army offensive operations from September 2015 to March 2016, a chronological look at the Russian Aerospace Group operations from late October 2015-March 2016, with specifics of Su-24M operations when available, the combat loss of a Russian Su-24M on 24 November 2015, and its aftermath.

It is beyond the scope of this volume to attempt an in-depth analysis of the Syrian conflict, which was in its fifth year before the Russian intervention in 2015. However, a brief outline of the situation on the ground in certain areas is provided where relevant to the Russian campaign as well as a brief outline of the differences in the Russian and western dominated anti-ISIS coalition approach to the attempt to defeat ISIS forces, which, in early 2017, remained entrenched in much of Syria.

All technical information concerning the aircraft and weapons systems, along with the majority of the graphic material, has been furnished by the respective Design Bureaus and the Ministry of Defence of the Russian Federation.

Within the text there are variations in written orthography of place names such as Latakia, which is also laid-down as Lattakia, or Raqqa which is also laid-down as Raqqah in some texts. Predominantly references to Islamic State are laid down as ISIS.

1

THE SYRIAN CIVIL WAR – RUSSIA INTERVENES

The Russian Federation commenced offensive air operations over Syria on 30 September 2015, when, in response to a request for assistance from the government of the Syrian Arab Republic, the Aerospace Group, which had been forming at Hmeymim air base over the previous few weeks, formally commenced combat operations against ISIS (Islamic State of Iraq and the Levant) and other groups it deemed to be terrorist organisations embroiled in the Syrian civil war.

By summer 2015, civil war had raged within the Syrian Arab Republic for over four years, ever more external participants being drawn in as various groups and nations began picking at the bones of a nation in turmoil. It would certainly not be an understatement to say that going into summer 2015 things were looking bleak for the regime of Syrian President, Bashar al Assad, which was fighting on several fronts against many enemies and faced a growing threat from western powers sensing an opportunity to replace the regime with a western backed government despite the failures of such policies in Iraq, Afghanistan and Libya, all three countries being in the throes of turmoil following Anglo-US and other NATO (North Atlantic Treaty Organisation) nation campaigns and invasions, which had resulted in abject failure in that all three examples left those countries in lawless states of civil war, and, particularly in the case of Iraq and Libya, leading to the rise of extremist organizations like ISIS, which garnered much support from a populace that had been subjected to tyranny from their own governments and, in the case of Iraq, more than two decades of bombing and invasion by the major western powers.

The rise of ISIS beaconed black tidings for Syria as it advanced within that nation's borders taking ground previously held by government forces and the western backed so called 'moderate opposition'. By late summer, Syrian government forces had yielded some 20% of Syria's land mass to ISIS, which appeared all conquering, the moderate opposition, backed financially and to a certain degree with armament supplies from the coalition and other partner nations, taking advantage of the government forces fight against ISIS to try and make ground or consolidate ground already held, but also losing ground to ISIS at the same time.

The headaches for the Syrian regime were increasing almost daily, the anti-ISIS coalition, which commenced air operations against ISIS over Syria in September 2014, taking on more of a political anti-Assad coalition than a viable military strike force. It, of course, being an open secret within the populace of the countries involved that the ultimate aim was the overthrow of the Assad regime, despite the fact that Syrian government forces were the main bulwark against ISIS within Syria. Initially, it is inferred, it was hoped that the coalition air operation would provoke a response from the Syrian Arab Republic Air Force, which would then be engaged, followed by air strikes on Syrian air bases to neutralize its air power. With no such response arising from the Syrian air force, which, with its obsolete collection of combat aircraft, was in no position to counter the numerically overwhelming and technologically advanced air power arrayed against it, frustration within the coalition was leading to increasing talk about the imposition of a no NFZ (No Fly Zone), illegal under international law without the explicit authorisation of a UN resolution, but no less effective without. Such a NFZ would have given the coalition the pretext to shoot down Syrian aircraft regardless of any threat; the imposition of such a NFZ having no adverse effect on ISIS operations as that organization possessed absolutely no air power whatsoever. On the contrary, the imposition of a NZF would have been the greatest support the western powers could have afforded to ISIS as it would have prevented the Syrian government forces employing air power against superior ISIS forces on the ground. The proposed NFZ, which would have been directed entirely at the Syrian government forces, would, it is inferred, have, as was seen in Libya a short time before, evolved into an all-out air interdiction campaign against Syrian government forces, paving the way, not for the so called 'moderate' opposition forces, which were divided and incapable of operating as a cohesive military force, but ISIS, to advance on and overrun government held areas; in effect the Anti-ISIS coalition would have provided the very air support that would have allowed ISIS to defeat the Syrian government forces; the supposition being that the coalition would then turn fully on ISIS in support of the moderate opposition – the end game for Syria being decades of rule by a number of extremist organisations controlling various areas of the country.

On top of the threat of air attack by western powers, the Syrian government was faced with attacks by Turkey in support of opposition forces, often stated to include elements of ISIS, which had ambitions of carving out areas of northern Syria for incorporation into a greater Turkey or a self-styled Turkish controlled protectorate. Other members of the anti-ISIS coalition, including Saudi Arabia, were widely reported to be planning a ground invasion of eastern Syria, assumedly through some corridor in western Iraq or through Jordan, any such moves obviously requiring permission from the respective governments of those nations; Iraq already heavily embroiled in its own fight against ISIS with the political, material and military support of Iran and the political material support of Russia, as well as political, material military air support of the anti-ISIS coalition, the latter proving of enormous assistance in some areas. However, the air campaign was seriously flawed in that such air support was not forthcoming in support of Iranian supported Iraqi militias fighting ISIS. Any ground operation in Syria by Saudi forces would in all probability have ended in failure, the armed forces of that Kingdom unlikely to be capable of any meaningful sustained ground operation in the face of determined resistance without the support of western nations.

The Russian Federation, for her part, saw the preservation of the Assad regime as the surest way to defeat ISIS on the ground in Syria, there being no other alternative as the so called 'moderate opposition forces lacked the capability for such a campaign. Even supported by air power from the anti-ISIS coalition, the moderate opposition was, for the most part, coming up wanting when faced with determined opposition from ISIS forces. Their inability to contribute significantly to the offensive fight against ISIS, combined with their operations against government forces, which succeeded in drawing government forces away from the fight against ISIS, caused no little annoyance in Russia, which held the view that such groups were part of the greater extremist threat to Syria – drawing government forces away from the fight against ISIS effectively allied the 'moderate opposition' with that very same extremist threat to the Syrian Arab Republic.

It was clear within Russia that the main aim of the self-styled anti-ISSI coalition appeared to be the overthrow of the Syrian President, Bashar Al Assad. The above mentioned threat of extending airstrikes to Syrian government forces embroiled in the fight against ISIS and the threat of a ground invasion being the driving force behind Russia's decision to intervene in the conflict; the presence of Russian forces fighting alongside Syrian government forces would, it was clear, to all intents and purposes remove these threats.

As Russia began positioning forces at bases in western Syria towards late summer 2015, it had become clear that it planned some sort of military operation. The western powers assumed that it would merely be a show of force to thwart the coalition's plans for an attack against Syrian government forces, it being clear from that point onwards that this was no longer an option as it risked sparking a wider war against Russia which was clearly sending a signal that it intended to support its middle-east ally in the fight against extremism and any sustained attack by a western coalition. It remained now to be seen what Russia's intentions were as it garnered its air striking power that would be employed over Syria - the tactical combat aircraft of the Russian Aerospace Group based at Hmeymim air base, Latakia in western Syria. These air assets included Sukhoi Su-24M strike aircraft, Su-34 multifunctional strike fighters, Su-25SM ground attack aircraft and Su-30SM multidimensional strike fighters supported by UAV (Uninhabited Air Vehicle) and armed helicopters, the latter used for base protection and aircrew recovery in the event of an aircraft loss and the former used for surveillance, target verification and strike assessment among other roles. As the campaign progressed, these in theatre assets would be reinforced with additional Su-34's and, from early February 2016, a small detachment of Su-35S $4^{th}++$ generation multidimensional strike fighters; these latter aircraft assumed to have been deployed to counter the then increasing air threat inherent within the NATO command structure, particularly from Turkey.

Also at the disposal of the Russian Federation political and military command structure from day one was air and naval strike assets not in theatre, not least of which was the Kalibr-NK cruise missiles carried by Russian submarines and surface warships and air launched cruise missiles carried by the Tu-160 and Tu-95MS strategic missile carriers as well as the striking power provided by Long Range Aviation's Tu-22M3 long range bomber Divisions.

Unbeknownst to the western powers Russia had set a date of 30 September for the commencement of offensive air operations over Syria. Prior to the commencement of the its combat operation Russia had attempted to open chains of communication regarding the sharing of intelligence information concerning ISIS facilities and dispositions with the US and its coalition partners, but this was rejected, a move seen within Russia and some regional powers as destroying any pretense that the coalition air operations over Syria had been anything more than an opening move ultimately aimed at expending air operations against Syrian government forces.

An International Information Centre of Coordination Committee was set up by Russia, Syria, Iraq and Iran, the three latter nation's, at the time, most heavily embroiled in the fight against ISIS, ergo, being best placed to garner direct, on the ground, intelligence about ISIS dispositions and operations.

Even prior to the Russian intervention on 30 September 2015, the western powers had lost any initiative they thought they had in Syria; ISIS appearing to be all advancing. While voices in Washington and London were outspoken against Russia's position from the start, the Russian operation had much support throughout the wider world, but more importantly it had almost overwhelming support from most countries bordering or near to Syria, which would be most affected by an ISIS controlled Syria. Iraq, embroiled in its own fight against ISIS, gave permission for Russian aircraft to overfly its territory on ferry and transport flights to Syria as well as strike missions by aircraft emanating from Russia and cruise missiles launched from Russian warships cruising in the Caspian Sea or launched from Russian aircraft within Iranian airspace. Israel tacitly supported the operation, knowing all too well that, in the then current climate, the only viable alternative to the Assad regime in Syria was an Islamic State that would be anything but friendly to Israel. Jordan supported the operation, going on to host a coordination centre for Russian Syrian operations in Amman. Egypt expressed its support for the operation and the UAE (United Arab Emirates), which was operating as part of the anti-ISIS coalition, appeared to embrace the Russian operation as that nation and Russia both opposed a common enemy – ISIS. In the immediate region, Turkey and Saudi Arabia expressed hostility to the Russian operation, Saudi Araba's statements sounding like they could have been scripted in Washington or London, the United States and the United Kingdom's outspoken comments against Moscow being to a large extent outshone by the outright hostile comments and actions of Turkey towards the Russian operation.

2

SUKHOI Su-24M STRIKE AIRCRAFT

Together with the modern 4th+ generation Sukhoi Su-34 multifunctional strike fighter, the main in theatre strike element at the disposal of the Russian Aerospace Group operating in the Syrian Arab Republic was the Sukhoi Su-24M variable geometry strike aircraft. The Su-24M was in the process of being partially replaced in Russian service by the aforementioned Su-34. Despite being a dated design, dating back to the 1960/1970's, a number of Su-24M aircraft had been put through a limited upgrade program to keep the design viable as a strike platform until it could be completely replaced in Russian Federation service sometime in the 2020's.

The Su-24MK export variant was operated by the Syrian Arab Republic Air Force. these aircraft, which were less capable than their Russian counterparts, being employed on operations against ISIS and other opposition forces for several years before the Russian intervention in September 2015, several such aircraft being lost to ground defences within Syria and Israel as well as unknown numbers on the ground.

The genesis of the Su-24 design goes back to 1961, the Sukhoi Su-7B ground attack fighter, which was a relatively unsophisticated day attack aircraft, having officially entered service with the air forces of the USSR (Union of Soviet Socialist Republics) on 24 January 1961 that year. That same year, Sukhoi was instructed to commence design work on an enhanced variant of the Su-7, capable of day/night and adverse weather attack operations against a diversity of target sets ranging from relatively large fixed targets down to small battlefield size targets. This effectively laid the bedrock upon which the design groundwork commenced that would eventually lead to the Sukhoi T-6 that would in turn lead to the production first generation Su-24 and subsequently to the modern day Su-24M all-weather day/night strike aircraft.

Concept studies, designated S-28 and S-32, conducted at Sukhoi OKB New Projects Department during the course of 1961-1962, confirmed that it was not feasible to design a strike aircraft with the required capability simply by redesigning the Su-7, the major problem being the reality concerning the lack of available space required to house the extensive equipment required for the new strike aircraft.

The Su-24M, which was an evolution of the first generation Su-24, was developed in a number of variants during the 1980's, going on to serve with the air forces of the Soviet Union and later the Russian Federation. KnAAPO

As well as designing a new airframe, it was decided that a new generation of advanced (for the time) systems would be designed for the projected strike aircraft, including a new ANS (Aiming and Navigation System). This would be designed to allow, as stated in Sukhoi documentation, "automatic control over all major flight and tactical deployment procedures…" Leninets SPA (then known as OKB-794) was contracted to develop the ANS, allocated the code name 'Puma', under the design leadership of chief designer Ye.A. Zazorin.

As the Su-7B redesign option was considered a no-go, Sukhoi began work on a completely new design designated S-6, which was described in Sukhoi documentation as having a "standard aerodynamic configuration with a thin tapered wing featuring moderate sweepback, with two R-21F-300 type engines, developed by N.G. Metsvarishvili, and lateral variable air intakes with a horizontal airbrake. The crew of two (pilot and navigator/weapon system officer) were seated in the cockpit in tandem, one behind the other."

The S-6 conceptual design was completed in 1963, a full scale mock-up being produced that same year, but, following an air forces commission review, all major work on the program was suspended due to non-progression of design work on the Puma ANS. Work, however, recommenced in 1964, the program now being referred to under the Sukhoi code designation T-58M, indicating that design work now leant towards a modernised variant of the Sukhoi Su-15 interceptor (Sukhoi code T-58).

The new design focus was intended to lead to development of a low-altitude ground attack aircraft, the Soviet air forces performance requirements being altered significantly to cater for a design featuring STOL (Short Take-Off and Landing) capability and sustained supersonic flight whilst flying at low-altitude in order to enable the aircraft to be capable of penetrating defended airspace, this latter requirement being stated as of significant importance to the Soviet air forces. The aircraft still retained a tandem cockpit layout, but in 1965 the design team moved to a side-by-side seating arrangement, due, it was stated in Sukhoi documentation to the "increased cross dimension of the Orion sighting station antenna in the nose section of the fuselage." The design was to be powered by two S.K. Tumansky Design Bureau R-27F-300 derivative afterburning turbojets, complemented by four P.A. Kolesov Design Bureau RD-36-35 derivative lift booster engines to allow the required STOL capability.

Sukhoi converted T-58D-1, the first prototype of the Su-15 interceptor, to a flying laboratory configuration under the designation T-58VD with the R-27F-300/RD-36-35 powerplant combination. This aircraft was flight tested in this configuration by Sukhoi test pilot Ye. S. Solovyov during the period 1966-1969.

A decree of the Soviet government, dated 24 August 1965, had given the program team its official authorisation to develop the new strike aircraft, which was allocated the designation T-6. The conceptual design configuration and a design mock-up were approved in March 1966, leading to a detailed design phase, which was completed by the end of 1966.

Previous page and above: The Sukhoi OKB T6-1 (T-6-1) experimental STOL strike aircraft, which flew for the first time on 2 July 1967. Sukhoi

Two test vehicles were ordered, a static example for ground testing and one flight-rated aircraft for flight testing. This latter aircraft, designated T-6-1, was completed in May 1967, following which it entered into a ground test phase in preparation for its maiden flight, which took place from the FRI airfield on 2 July 1967 (pilot being Sukhoi chief test pilot V.S. Ilyushin), the aircraft having been transferred to the airfield on 29 June followed by airfield ground runs taking place on 1 July.

The T-6-2 was in effect the prototype of the Su-24 design. Sukhoi

The T-6-1 had been entered for participation in the Domodedovo air display that was scheduled to take place on 9 July 1967, but any hopes of this were dashed when the aircraft was damaged in an accident, the left side opening of the canopy having been torn of its hinging during its second flight on 4 July. The aircraft was brought to a successful emergency landing. Modifications to the canopy were conducted and the aircraft conducted its third flight the next day, 5 July.

The initial flight test series was conducted minus the RD-36-35 lift boosters, which were installed in October 1967 during the programs engineering follow up phase, which also saw the R-27 turbojets replaced by A.M. Lyulka AL-21F afterburning turbojets. Installation of the lift boosters allowed STOL testing to be conducted between November 1967 and January 1968. The findings, combined with the results of the STOL testing conducted on the T-58VD, confirmed that the improved take-off and landing performance did not justify the reduced range of the planned strike aircraft, attributed, among other things, to increased fuel consumption due to the excess weight of the four RD-36-35 lift boost engines. The lift boosters imposed other penalties on the aircraft, which, as stated in Sukhoi Design Bureau documentation, included "hazardous impact of the exhaust gases on the plane's structural members and landing gear, the impossibility of suspending external stores and ordnance from the bottom of the fuselage. The aeroplane's pronounced overbalancing in the forward lift axis upon their activation." It was clear that the advantages of the lift boosters were far outweighed by the disadvantages, therefore, they were dropped, the design team looking at alternative ways to improve take-off and landing performance.

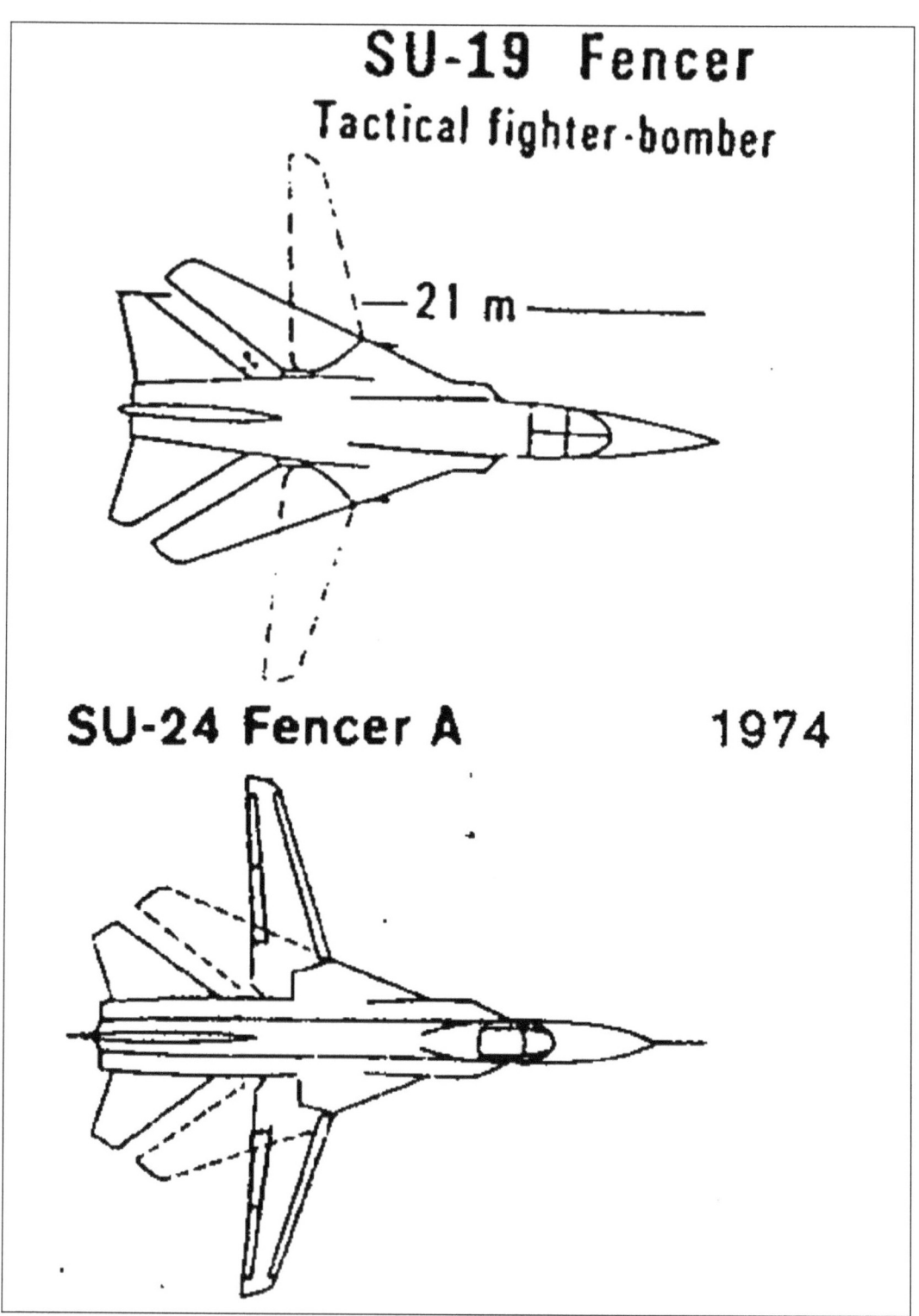

Western intelligence inferences of the layout of the Su-24 from 1972 (the aircraft was thought to have been designated Su-19 at this time) and 1974 were inaccurate in detail, but provided a generalisation of the aircraft external characteristics.

Around mid-1967, Sukhoi had commenced studies into a variable geometry (swing wing) configuration for the T-6. This, combined with the later decision to drop the lift boosters, leading to a new design being put forward, authorisation for which was given in a decree of the Soviet Government dated 7 August 1968. The preliminary design was, as stated in Sukhoi documentation, "finalised by the air force as an addendum to the 1965 requirements." The redesigned T-6 was completed during the period 1968 to 1969, two prototypes being built by autumn of the latter year. The first of the flight test prototypes, T-6-2, was transferred to the Sukhoi Design Bureau flight test and development facility at the FRI airfield on 10 November 1969. There followed an extensive ground test phase in preparation for its maiden flight, which took place on 17 January 1970 when Sukhoi chief test pilot V.S. Ilyushin lifted the aircraft off the runway, commencing a four year flight program over several phases that lasted into July 1974.

The construction process for the aircraft exterior included the use of lengthy machined panels. The basic design features of the T-6 included, as stated in Sukhoi documentation, "a variable-geometry shoulder wing, which gave the areophane acceptable TOLC and superior APC in various flight modes." The side-by-side seating arrangement of its predecessor was retained in the T-6, the crew of two being seated on K-36D zero-zero ejection seats, facilitating the possibility of escape from the aircraft in the event of an emergency even when the aircraft was on the ground.

The T-6-2 was developed for service as the Su-24. Sukhoi

The T-6-2, like all future variants of the Su-24, was powered two AL-21 afterburning turbojet engines developed by A.M. Lyulka. JSC Salut

Airframe aside, at the heart of the new strike aircraft's capabilities was the Puma ANS, incorporating a modern day JSC OKB Electroautomatics Orbita-10-58 computer system, which included two separate, superimposed, Orion-A radar antenna's for the functions of navigation and attack, combined with a Relyef terrain clearance (referred to in the west as terrain avoidance or terrain following) radar which could perform an automatic control of flight profiles down to ultra-low altitudes. The Orion-A system had an effective range out to around 150 km.

The Orbita system had been developed to supersede the FDC 263 first generation TSR on-board computer developed to provide precise navigation for the reconnaissance variant of the MiG-25 and the 'Puma' system developed for the T-6. Such first generation systems were encumbered with a large mass, the excessive weight being a considerable problem for tactical fighter size aircraft, effectively restricting their use to that of ground testing the equipment and software required in the developmental path towards a digital computer system, the first generation of which was the 'Orbita-1' on-board computer of dynamic micro-modules PI-64 and PI-65.

A retired Su-24 on display at NAPO (Novosibirsk Aircraft Plant, Chkalov). NAPO

The new strike aircraft design could be armed with a variety of air to surface missiles including the Kh-23 and Kh-28 guided missiles as well a variety of free fall unguided bombs. For self defence against airborne threats the R-55 short-range IR (Infrared) guided air to air missiles was specified.

Series production of the T-6 design commenced in 1971. The Yuri Gargarin Komsomolsk-on-Amur production plant in the Soviet Far East, under the directorship of V.Ye. Kopylov, assembled the rear fuselage/tail units, including the vertical tail, and the wing panels. The Novosibirsk plant manufactured the forward and centre fuselage units and the centre wing sections, final assembly taking place at this location.

The first series production T-6 conducted its maiden flight (pilot, chief test pilot V.T. Vylomov) from the Novosibirsk test facility on 31 December 1971. Deliveries of production aircraft to the Soviet air forces commenced in 1973 when the 4th APCT&TTC (Airborne Personnel Combat Training and Transition Training Centre) at Voronezh began receiving aircraft for training purposes. The first combat unit to receive the new strike aircraft was the 3rd Bomber Regiment located at Chernyakhovsk air base in the Baltic Military District.

The T-6 was officially accepted into the inventory of the Soviet air forces, under the service designation of Su-24, by a decree of the Soviet government dated 4 February 1975. Stage 1 of service testing, utilising the 3rd Bomber Regiment, was conducted between May 1975 and August 1976, followed by Stage 2 service testing, utilising the Bomber Regiment of the Transcaucasian Military District, from January 1981 until March 1982. Production of the first generation Su-24 continued until 1983.

Top: Su-24 with the variable-geometry wings at intermediate sweep. Above: **Su-24 with main and nose undercarriage extended.** US DoD

The first generation Su-24 could be considered as an interim model to expedite service entry whilst development of a more capable variant, which commenced in the early 1970's, was conducted. The improved variant would be equipped with an in-flight refueling probe, developed by 1971. Mission effectiveness would be significantly improved by incorporation of a new attack system and by increasing the available weapon load which included the new generation of air to surface missiles such as the Kh-29T/L and Kh-58 along with 500 kg and 1500 kg class KAB guided bomb units. The R-60 short-range infrared guided air to air missile replaced the obsolete R-55 missile for self-defence against threat aircraft. In 1983, conceptual work commenced on equipping the T-6 with an enhanced detection and targeting capability courtesy of a Kaira TV (Television) optical quantum system along with a pod mounted Tekon search and tracking system for use with the Kh-59/Kh-59M TV guided air to surface missile. The various improvements to the new design were estimated to increase combat effectiveness by a factor of between 1.5 and 2 times compared with that of the first generation Su-24.

The T-6M-8, referred to as an aerodynamic development aircraft, was in effect the prototype of the Su-24M. Sukhoi

To accommodate new equipment the new variant of the T-6, designated T-6M, emerged with a nose section of increased length. Much of the new equipment for the T-6M was flight tested on first generation T-6 aircraft, the T-6M-8, referred to as an aerodynamic development aircraft, conducting its maiden flight on 29 June 1977, followed by the maiden flight of the first of two pre-production T-6M's from Novosibirsk on 17 December that year (crew consisting of chief test pilot V.T. Vylomov and Navigator A.N. Kosarev).

Development flight testing of the T-6M was conducted from December 1976 through into May 1981, the first series production T-6M having conducted its maiden flight on 20 June 1979 (crew consisting of pilot V.T. Vylomov and navigator G.V. Gridusov). Production of the new variant was initially set up along the same lines as that of the first generation Su-24, being shared between Komsomolsk-on-Amur and Novosibirsk. However, it was later, around mid-1980, transferred in its entirety to Novosibirsk (this also being effective for the first generation Su-24 then still in production) due to Komsomolsk's increased workload with production of the Su-27 4th generation air superiority fighter at the plant.

An early production Su-24M configured with fuselage and wing mounted stores. Sukhoi

The Soviet air forces began receiving series production T-6M's, with the service designation of Su-24M, when a number of aircraft were delivered to the 4th CEV at Voronezh in June 1981, the design being declared in service with the air forces of the Soviet Union by a decree of the Soviet government dated 22 June 1983. Service testing commenced in 1985 and continued into 1986. Production of the Su-24M continued until 1993.

The first generation Su-24 was equipped with a Chaika system, which was a simple daytime use only optical sight. An emitter detection system, referred to as Filin, which was located under the optical sight, was employed to provide targeting information to the Kh-28 anti-radiation missile. In the Su-24M the Chaika system was replaced by a Kaira-24M system developed from the Kaira-1 system fitted in the Mikoyan (Now RSK MiG) MiG-27 variable-geometry ground attack/fighter. This system, with a ± 35° field of view and a +6°/-180° elevation with a range out to 12 km, was located on the Su-24M underside.

In Soviet and later Russian service, the Su-24 was equipped with a SPO-15 RWR (Radar Warning Receiver) L006, which provided 360° coverage; development of this system dating back to the late 1960's/early 1970's. A Geran jamming system, initially an SPS-161, L101, system known as Geran-F and later an SPS-162, L102, installed on later production aircraft, was incorporated to enable jamming of systems in the 6-12 Ghz frequency bands, these systems being outmoded by the late 1990's. The Su-24M Self-defence suite also included an L082 Mak-UL IR (Infrared) missile approach warning system.

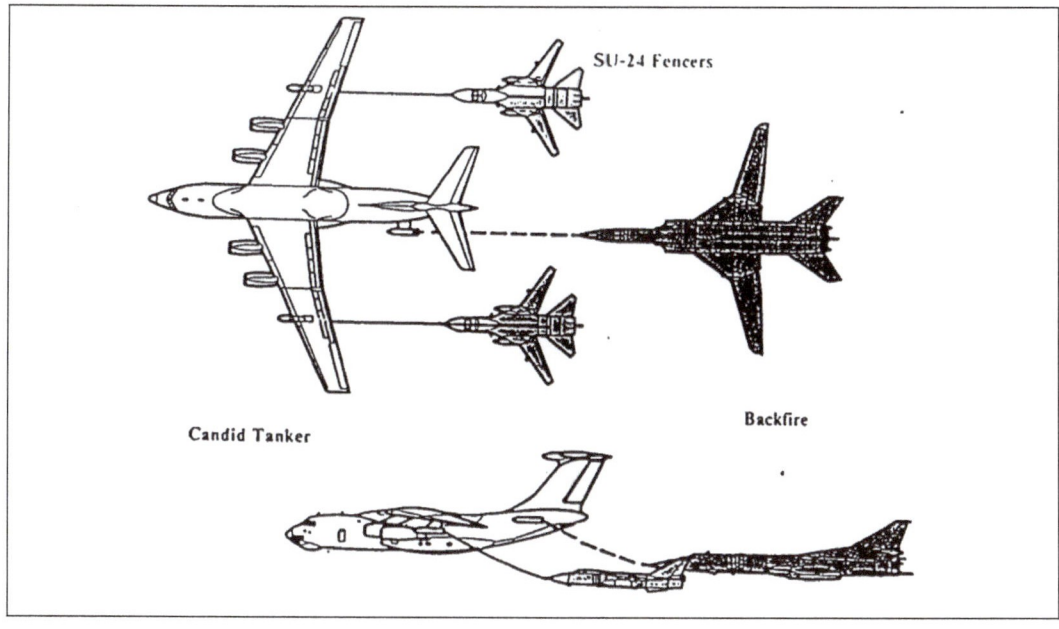

The Su-24M could employ in-flight refueling to extend mission radius. As well as receiving fuel in-flight the Su-24M could be employed as a buddy tanker (top), in which it could be equipped with a fuselage centerline mounted refilling unit to pass fuel to receiver aircraft, most notably other Su-24M's. Rostec Corporation **The diagram (above) shows Su-24 aircraft refueling from wing hose units on an Il-78 tanker aircraft with a Tu-22M intermediate-range bomber refueling from the rear fuselage refueling unit.** US Gov

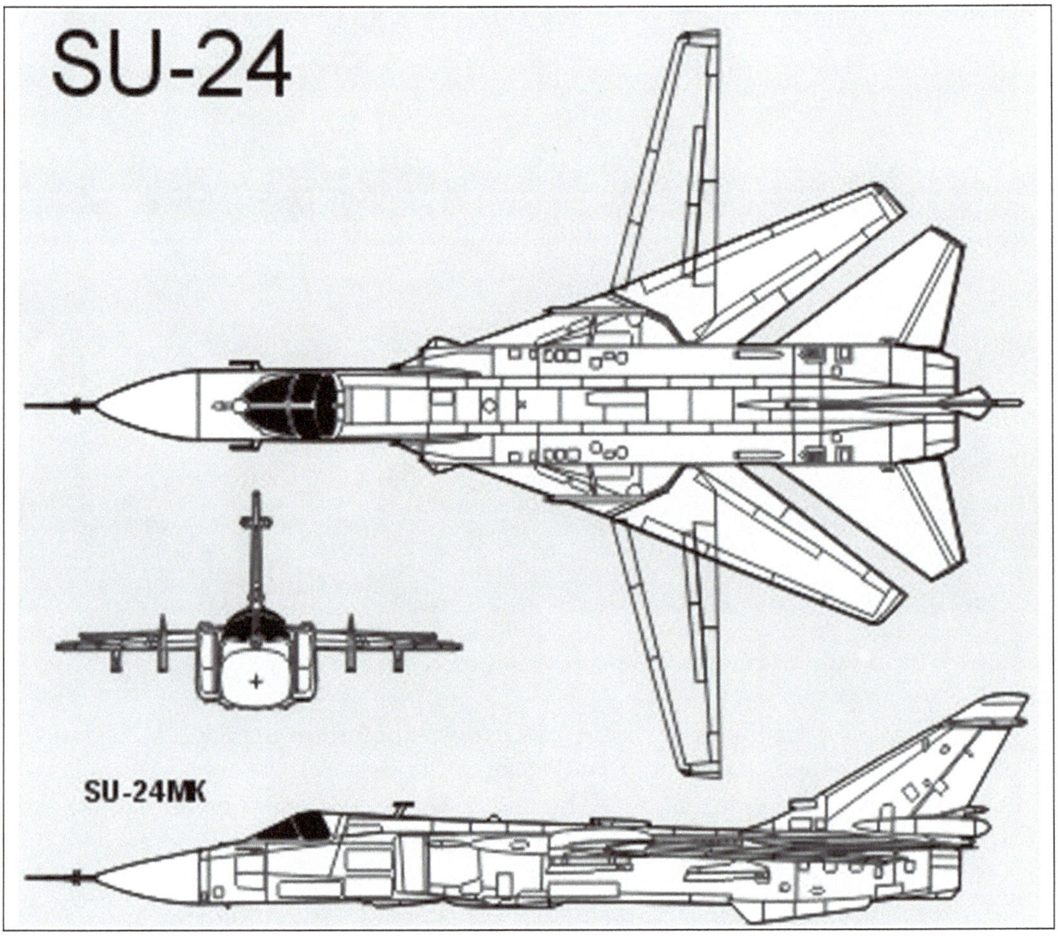

Top: A Su-24M of Soviet Naval Aviation over the Baltic Sea in company with a Su-27 4th generation fighter. Above: General arrangement 3-view drawing of the export Su-24MK, which was also representative of the Su-24M. NAPO

Above: A Su-24MK Fencer D developed for export. NAPO/PVO

An export variant of the Su-24M, the Su-24MK (T-6MK), was developed, this variant conducting its maiden flight on 30 May 1987 (crew consisting of pilot Ye.N. Rudakas and navigator V.V. Rudakov). The Su-24MK, which differed from the domestic Su-24M only in certain items of avionics and equipment fit, entered series production, the first example of which was flown on 17 May 1988. Between then and 1992 deliveries were made to Algeria, Libya, Iran, Iraq and Syria.

Su-24MP electronic warfare development aircraft. Sukhoi

A number of special mission variants were developed from the Su-24M, including the T-6MR (reconnaissance) and T-6MP (electronic warfare), these being developed from earlier studies designated T-58MR and T-58MP, the initial design studies for which had been completed in 1973 before the programs went into abeyance as the T-6M airframe design was being refined. Re-emerging in 1976 as the T-6MR and T-6MP, prototypes for which were built from converted T-6M airframes. The T-6MP-25 development aircraft conducted its maiden flight on 14 March (pilot, Komarov) and the T-6MR-26 development aircraft conducted its maiden flight on 25 July 1980 (pilot, A.A. Ivanov). Development of both variants, which was conducted concurrently, was completed in November 1982.

Top: Su-24MR reconnaissance variant development aircraft. Sukhoi **Above: Su-24MR Yellow 40 of the newly established Russian Federation Air Force at RAF Leuchars, Scotland in September 1992** Author

The first series production T-6MP, allocated the service designation Su-24MP, conducted its maiden flight from Novosobirsk on 7 April 1983 (pilot I.Ya. Sushko and navigator V.Ya. Glinchikov), production totaling ten units only. The first series production T-6MR, allocated the service designation Su-24MR, conducted its maiden flight on 13 April 1983 (pilot V.T. Vylomov and navigator V.S. Shkuratov), six days after the maiden flight of the Su-24MP. Production of the Su-24MR continued until 1993, aircraft being allocated to a number of Aviation Reconnaissance Regiments in the various Soviet and later Russian Military Districts. The first unit to receive this variant was the 4th APCT&TC, which received its first example in summer 1983. The first operational unit to receive the MR variant was the 47th SGRAR of MMD of Air Forces (Shatalovo), which was responsible for service testing between 1987 and 1988.

Production of all Su-24 variants, developed under the design leadership of Ye. S. Felsner from 1965 to 1985 and then L.A. Logvinov from 1985, was in the order of 1,400 units.

The Su-24/M has been used operationally in a number of theatres, most notably, in regards to domestic operators, being their operational employment by the Soviet Union in Afghanistan in the 1980's and by the Russian Federation Air Force in Chechnya in the 1990's and again in the Russian intervention to repel the Georgian attack on South Ossetia in 2008, and, of course over Syria from September 2015.

Serious proposals for an Su-24M/MK modernisation were mooted in the late 1990's and early 2000's, the model above showing an aircraft armed with R-73E short-range IR guided air to air missiles and Kh-31 air to surface missiles, which would be available in a number of variants, including the Kh-31A anti-ship missile and Kh-31P anti-radiation missile. Author

Three views of a Su-24M 3-D animation. MODRF

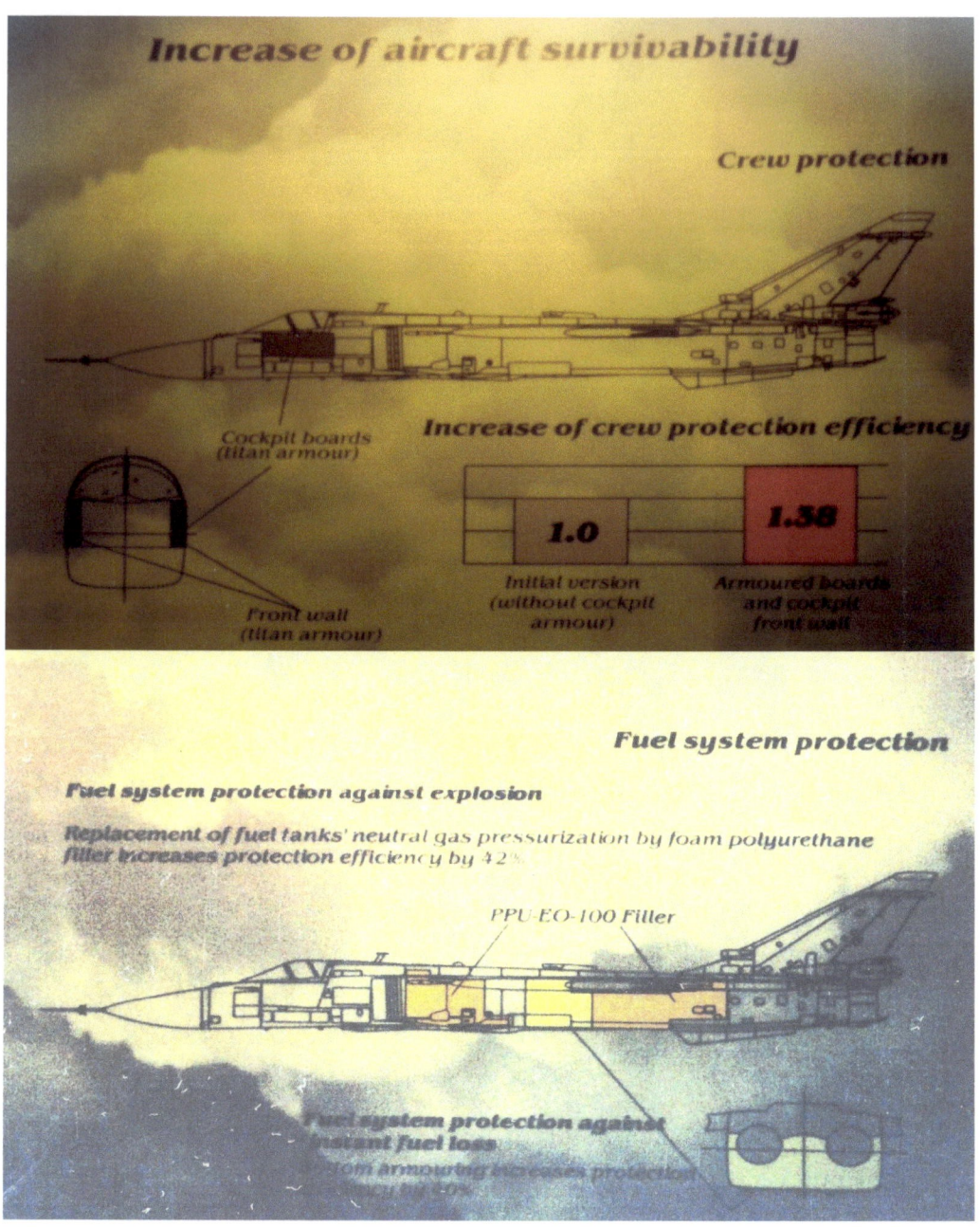

Graphics, dating back to 2001, for proposals for various survivability upgrade options, not implemented, for the Su-24M/MK. Author

An Su-24M upgrade, relatively modest in scope and implementation, was aimed at improving the capabilities of a portion of the Russian Federation Su-24M fleet whilst the Su-34 4th+ multifunctional strike fighter was under development as a replacement for at least part of the Su-24M fleet. The main elements of the upgrade were intended to enhance the existing ANS by replacing obsolete computing systems with modern systems, installing an INS (Inertial Navigation System) and GPS

(Global Positioning System) navigation system with associated displays and enhancing the weapons employment capability by introducing a number of new weapons and increasing the delivery accuracy for unguided weapons. The cockpit was transformed with a number of colour MFDS (Multi-Function Display Screens) replacing a plethora of dials and controls.

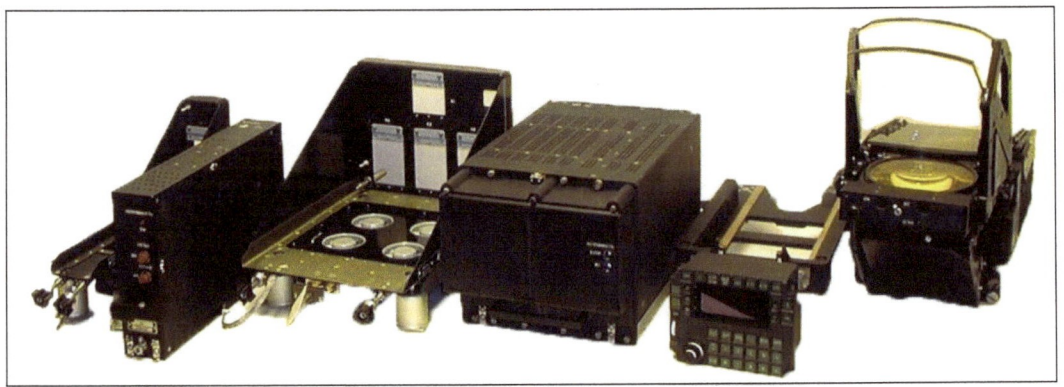

Modernised Su-24M's are equipped with the JSC Electroavtomatica SDI-24 Information Display System dominated by the BI HUD display unit. JSC Electroavtomatica

The upgrade package to be implemented was finalised in 2005, two Su-24M's later being delivered to JSC Sukhoi subsidiary NAPO (Novosibirsk Aircraft Production Association) for implementation to commence. A quartet of Su-24M's, having received some enhancements, were by that time already operating from the CCTC (Combat Conversion Training Centre) at Lipetsk, these, it is inferred, having been operated, at least to a degree, in support of the upgrade program for 24 Algerian Su-24MK's to Su-24MK2 standard at NAPO, which was completed in 2005.

On 15 August 2006, the first two upgraded Su-24M's were delivered from NAPO's Novosibirsk facility to the Russian Federation Air Force. The aircraft were flown the short distance to the CCTC at Lipetsk where they underwent trials. It also appears that two Su-24M2's were delivered to Lipetsk on 7 December 2015, it being probable that these were the same aircraft as above, one of the dates being wrong. Another possibility is that the first two aircraft, being trials aircraft, were not part of the initial upgrade contract of six operational aircraft outlined below. While other aircraft were being upgraded, a number of crews were sent to Lipetsk to work up on the new variant, the last of the six aircraft to be upgraded under the initial contract being completed in November 2007. Four of these aircraft were apparently delivered to Pereyaslavka air base, near to Khabarovsk, on 24 December 2007.

A further six Su-24M's were transferred from Pereyaslavka to NAPO for upgrade in line with plans to modernise 20 such aircraft from the Regiment based there. It is unclear how many Russian Federation Air Force Su-24M's were eventually upgraded to M2 standard, but it is unlikely to more than several tens of aircraft as increasing numbers of Su-34 strike aircraft have come online (some 100 by the end of 2016) in the past half-decade or so, this latter type entering operational service in 2014.

Modernised Su-24M2/MK2 aircraft can be equipped with the KS-418E Electronic Warfare Complex designed to protect the host aircraft from radar guided air to air and surface to air missiles. None of the Russian Su-24's deployed to the Syrian Arab Republic in 2015 appeared to be equipped with the complex.

At the heart of the crew, seated on K-36 zero-zero ejection seats, cockpit environment is the JSC OKB Electroautomatics developed SDI-24 Information Display System for the Su-24. This system displays relevant tactical or flight information on a screen collimator indicator as well as repeating information on the control screen.

The single BFVI-24 visual information unit provides, as stated in JSC OKB Electroautomatics documentation, "reception and transmission of analog signals DC signals (15 inputs/outputs 7), serial code (34/10) and one-time commands (60/44), information exchange on the multiplex communication lines (2 channels), software processing of the received information; imaging mnemokadrov on BI [display console] with digital correction and signal deviation and illumination of the electron beam." The single BI display console repeats collimated navigation and plotting data. The BOO control block provides the system with a secondary power supply for the BFVI-24 and BI. An ISP-24 Control Panel controls in-flight data as an element of the overall 4280G8-10 Controller, which provides data reception and transmission (in-effect a data exchange and multiplex channel control unit). The system operates in the Russian and Latin alphabet. The ISP-24 control and display panel facilitates the entering and adjustment of the operational parameters of the aircraft flight and displays necessary flight information on a display scream. The other major elements of the system consist of 1 RM-24, 1 PM BU and 1 PM BI frame mountings.

Other advanced systems available to the Su-24M2/MK2 included the KS-418E EW (Electronic Warfare) complex designed to protect the host aircraft from radar directed threats such as radar guided air to air missiles. The system can function automatically even when offline and can counter several electronic threats simultaneously in pulsing and semi-continuous modes. It should be noted that there is no evidence to suggest that this system has been employed by Russian Federation Su-24M's operating over Syria in 2015/2016.

In 2016, although being supplanted by the modern 4th+ generation Su-34 multifunctional strike fighter, the Su-24M/M2 forms the numerical backbone of the tactical strike forces of the Russian Federation Air Force element of the Aerospace Forces, with some 250 aircraft in service (2015 values), a smaller number also operating with Russian naval aviation; these latter aircraft in the process of being replaced by Su-30SM 4th+ generation multidimensional strike fighters. The Su-24MK remains in service with Algeria, Iran and Syria, and a number of Su-30M's were allocated to former Soviet Republics, including Ukraine, on the break-up of the Soviet Union in 1991.

Su-24M/MK Specification – Data furnished by JSC Sukhoi

Powerplant: Two x AL-21FZA afterburning turbojet engines each rated at 11200 kg in afterburner
Length: 24.532 m
Wingspan: 17.638 m (fully swept forward) and 10.336 m (fully swept back)
Height: 6.193 m
Normal take-off weight: 28040 kg
Maximum take-off weight: 43755 kg
Maximum landing weight: 27900 kg
Maximum internal fuel capacity: 11100 kg
Normal stores load: 2000 kg
Maximum stores load: 8000 kg
Fixed armament: single 23 mm cannon with 500 rounds of ammunition
Maximum flight speed at sea level: 1315 km/h in clean configuration
Maximum Mach number in clean configuration: 1.35
Service ceiling: 11 km without external stores
Operational radius of action at sea level in mixed mode (Vcr in the 200 km area, V=900 km/h in other areas) with PTB external fuel tanks and 6 x FAB-500M-62 bombs: 615 km
Ferry flight range configured with 2 x PTB-3000 external fuel tanks: 2775 km if external tanks are dropped and 5000 km with one in-flight refueling
In-flight refueling system maximum flow rate (at entry pressure of 3.5 kg/cm^2): 1100 l/m
Take-off run at normal take-off weight: 1550 m
Landing run at normal take-off weight: (with employment of the braking parachute system): 1100 m
Crew: 2, pilot and navigator/weapon system operator

AL-31F – Data furnished by JSC Salut

The Su-24/Su-24M was powered by 2 x AL-21F afterburning turbojet engines, low rate serial production of which commenced in 1966. The AL-21F powered a number of aircraft designs, Su-17M, Su-22, MiG-23B, as well as the Su-24, mass serial production of the engine being initiated in 1972. A number of engines retired from flight status have been used to power industrial power generator stations and gas-transfer plants.

Maximum thrust: 11250 kgf
Inlet diameter: 885 mm
Maximum dimeter: 1030 mm
Length: 5340 mm
Maximum specific fuel consumption: 0.76 kg/kgf/h
Dry weight: 1580 kg
Air consumption: 104 kg/s

Avionics and sensor systems – Data furnished by JSC Sukhoi

Attack and Navigation System: includes digital computer, Doppler navigator, Optical sighting system, I/O device (I/O), OBS (On-board switchgear), photo recording system, control signal conditioner, on-board module of Tekon-1 television guidance system, LTVSTS (Laser/TV Search and Track System), radio command linkage and the passive radar system consisting of letter A and A' instrumentation pod, letter B and B' instrumentation pod, the NRS (Nose Radar Scanner), the CWR (Collision Warning Radar), small size inertial instrument system, low-range radio altimeter, NRS video signal onboard processing block. TV display and GPS satellite navigation system.

Other Elements of the avionics systems include the autopilot, IFF, VHF-UHF communications systems, short-wave radio, automatic detection finder and aircraft responder – long-range radio technical navigation system, short-range radio technical navigations system, flight data recorder, camera, tape-recording mechanism, solid state storage unit, combat performance monitoring equipment. VCR and a weapons control system.

The self-defence suite includes an ECM (Electronic Counter Measures) system, RWR (Radar Warning Receiver), jamming capabilities control device, active jamming system, IRSTS (Infrared Search and Tracking System), cartridge ejection mechanism (chaff/flare dispenser system) and integrated defensive aids suite.

BI HUD – data furnished by JSC Electroavtomatica

Full Field of vision: diameter 24°.
Instant field of vision: 17 x 17°.
Weight: 20 (unit unspecified but inferred to be kg)
Dimensions
Length x width x height: 505 x 213 x 376 mm
Interfaces: analog beam steering inputs
Functional design: display unit
Status: serial production for Su-24
Indicator: LED

Su-24 stores options can include – data furnished by JSC Sukhoi
Kh-25ML, Kh-25MR (Kh-23ML), Kh-28T/L, Kh-58E, Kh-58E-01 (lit. A, A, B, C), Kh-31P (lit. A, A', B, B', C), Kh-31A, Kh-59, Kh-59ME, S-25LD air to surface guided missiles, R-60 or R-73E infrared guided air to air missiles, KAB-500KR and KAB-500KL guided bomb units, AB-100, AB-250 (M54), AB-250 (M62), AB-500M-54, ODAB-500PM unguided bombs, RBK-250 and RBK-500 cluster bomb units, S-24B incendiary bomb, S-25OFM unguided rockets, SPPU-6 gun pods, KMGU-2 small size cargo pods and PTB-2000 (1860 l) and PTB-3000 (3050 l) external fuel tanks. External stores carried on 8 external stations

In operations over the Syrian Arab Republic Russian Su-24M's have employed the PTB-2000 (1860 l), one carried under each wing. The larger capacity PTB-3000 (3050 l) external fuel tanks do not appear to have been employed.

Weapons known to have been employed on operations during the period covered, either through confirmation by the MODRF (Ministry of Defence of the Russian Federation) or by visual identification through imagery, consist of the following: Kh-25ML laser guided air to surface missile, KAB-500 guided bomb unit, BETAB-500 concrete piercing bomb and the OFAB-250/270 HE fragmentation unguided bomb. There is no evidence that active radar guided Kh-25MAE/MSE missiles have been employed in operations over Syria and there has been no requirement for such weapons as the Kh-25MP Airborne Modular Tactical Guided Missiles optimised for the anti-radiation mission.

Kh-25ML

Serial production of the Kh-25 laser guided tactical missile commenced in 1975 following completion of state flight tests that had commenced on 24 November 1974. The Kh-25 entered service with the Soviet air forces in 1976.

The Kh-25 was one of a number of missile designs that were developed in modular form in that relatively common missile bodies would be produced with different interchangeable homing heads leading to the Kh-25M developed in three variants – Kh-25ML multi-purpose missile with laser seeker, Kh-25MR multi-purpose missile with radar guidance and Kh-25MP anti-radar missile with a passive radar homing head. Following completion of state tests of the Kh-25M modular missile systems series production commenced in 1982.

Kh-25ML – Data furnished by JSC Tactical Missiles Corporation

Launch range: up to 40 km (this value is for the radar guided variant, the ML having a shorter acquisition range)
Launch altitude parameters: 50-12000 m
Maximum speed: 920 km/h
Warhead type: High explosive or penetrating
Warhead weight: no more than 90 kg
Missile launch weight: radar guided variants have launch weights of 323 and 330 kg, it being inferred that the launch weight of the ML would be in this class)
Length: 4.355 m (value provided relates to the modernized MSE radar guided variant, but the ML is in a similar value range)
Diameter: 0.275 m
Wing span: 0.755 m

OFAB-250-270

The OFAB-250-270 is an unguided high-explosive blast fragmentation bomb widely employed by Russian tactical combat aircraft and Tu-22M3 intermediate range bombers. The weapon, which is designed to destroy soft and light armoured targets, weights 268 kg.

Top: OFAB-250-270 series bomb. Armaco **Above: A BETAB-500 concrete piercing bomb on a fuselage station of a Su-24M.** Rosoboronexport

Su-24M White 24 of the Russian Aerospace Group armed with BETAB-500 concrete piercing bombs on wing station during combat operations from Hmeymim air base in the Syrian Arab Republic in late 2015. MODRF

BETAB-500

Design of the BETAB-500 air bomb is intended for the destruction of reinforced concrete structures and fortifications. The weapon, which can be employed against a diversity of targets such as hardened aircraft and other ground shelters, airfield runways, major roadways and warships, is capable of penetrating reinforced concrete structures up to 1 m thick that have been covered with up to 3 m of normal ground compact soil.

OFAB-500-270 – Data furnished by Hartford International and Armaco

Length: 1456 mm
Diameter: 395 mm
Weight: 268 kg
Charge Weight: 92 kg

BETAB-500 – data furnished by Rosoboronexport

Diameter: 350 mm
Length: 2200 mm
Bomb weight: 477 kg
Explosive weight (TNT equivalent): 98 kg
Release altitude: 30-5000 m
Release speed: 600-1200 km/h

3

THE RUSSIAN AIR CAMPAIGN – THE OPENING PHASE

The Russian air campaign in the Syrian Arab Republic could be simplified into four main categories: tactical support to SDA (Syrian Democratic Army) ground forces conducting field operations against ISIS (Islamic State of Iraq and the Levant) forces and other opposition groups; infrastructure and supply route interdiction against ISIS and other opposition group occupied areas; oil infrastructure and transportation interdiction and air defence, the latter taking an increasingly visible role following NATO (North Atlantic Treaty Organisation) interference with the Russian operation in late November 2015. There were of course other areas of operations, not least of which was logistics resupply, air base defence and search and rescue.

The Russian air campaign was to be conducted within the Syrian command structure, a joint Russian/Syrian command centre being located at Hmeymim air base to this end. In the first days of the campaign the MODRF (Ministry of Defence of the Russian Federation) stated that Russian aircraft were only assigned targets that were "outside inhabited areas" (apparently a temporary measure due to the nature of the conflict being contested in towns and cities), these targets being attacked only once their validity had been confirmed by reconnaissance and other intelligence sources. The main reconnaissance tools at the Russian's disposal came in the shape of space based satellite reconnaissance and UAV (Uninhabited Air Vehicle), some 70 of the latter stated to have been operational in Syria by the end of February 2016.

On the morning of 30 September 2015, Russian General, Kuralenko, in person, notified the US (United States) Military attaché in Iraq, Colonel Petro, that Russia would commence strike missions over Syria later that day. Similarly, through a number of diplomatic and military channels of the MODRF and the Russian Ministry of Foreign Affairs, other parties were advised of the forthcoming operations and further advised to remove any personal they may have on the ground assisting various opposition groups, advisers or instructors; the US pledging that there were no US personnel in the areas Russia indicated its operations would take place. Russia further advised member states of the self-styled 'anti-ISIS' coalition to refrain from air operations in the areas that Russian indicated its operations would take place.

The major combat element of the Russian Aerospace Group deployed to Hmeymim air base in the Syrian Arab Republic in late summer 2015 consisted of Su-24M and Su-34 strike aircraft (previous page), Su-25SM ground attack aircraft (this page top) and Su-30SM multidimensional strike fighters (this page bottom). MODRF

The areas that Russia indicated to the 'anti-ISIS' coalition that its air strikes would take place appear to have been leaked, for even before the first Russian aircraft took-off on 30 September, media reports of civilian casualties began to appear, the sources, not being privy to the times of the air strikes, pre-empting slightly their actuality. These fabricated reports would permeate throughout the campaign creating a situation akin to the little boy who cried wolf, it being impossible to separate fabricated reports of civilian casualties from factual reports of civilian casualties, which, despite Russian reports to the contrary, there were almost certain to be a number, as there were with 'anti-ISIS' coalition strikes that resulted in civilian casualties. However, there is no information available to this writer that there were any deliberate attacks on civilians. Such actions would, of course, have been counterproductive in a campaign to overcome ground force operations that in many areas amounted to foreign invasions of the host country – the Syrian Democratic Republic.

As soon as the Russian campaign got underway a full-scale disinformation campaign got underway in western and western influenced countries. For example, in the (United Kingdom, on top of all the political rhetoric, the head of MI6 made public statements that may have been deigned to instill a sense that the Russian campaign in support of the Syrian government forces was directed primarily at the western backed opposition forces in an alliance with ISIS. Time proved this to be nothing more than fallacious vocal exercising, adding further mistrust of the intelligence services following the spate of dodgy dossiers produced in support of the Blair governments desire to invade Iraq, without justification, in 2003. What made this particular misinformation campaign all the more worrying was the fact that it was either supported by the majority of the western media, many of the reports of which came across as if they had been scripted by government speechmakers, such was the anti-Russian sentiment that was growing in the west as a result of ill thought out mistruths about Russian threats that had not been levelled. In the UK for instance there were numerous references to facing the threat from Russia, despite the fact that Russia had not threatened a single western nation nor any of its neighbors (there being two sides to the conflict in Ukraine, the Russian and Crimean population view that that the annexation of Crimea was justified in view of the undemocratic events transpiring in western Ukraine and the fact that Crimea was historically a part of Russia until gifted to Ukraine in 1954). Such disinformation campaigns were of course designed to instill public opinion in favour of the current NATO strategy of encircling Russia and increasing a military presence on Russia's borders, something that was refrained from even during the darkest days of the Cold War. An example of this being the fact that Norway, which had always refused to allow NATO forces other than its own national forces, to be stationed on Norwegian soil, even during the Cold-War, abandoned this policy in 2016 despite the lack of any newly emerged threat. On the contrary, Russia perceived this act as a threat to her own security, fueling the avalanche of mistrust that was gathering momentum with each passing month.

Previous page: Su-24M's, configured with external fuel tanks, operating from Hmeymim in the first days of the Russian air campaign. This page: Afterburner section of the AL-21F turbojet engine of a Su-24M at Hmeymim. Above: With a telltale smoke trail, an Su-24M approaches to land at Hmeymim air base. MODRF

The Russia air campaign was initiated under the auspices of its Aerospace Group based at Hmeymim air base in the northern Latakia province of Syria, although it would also call on other sea, land and air based assets, the latter based on Russian territory. Initially the Aerospace Group consisted of Sukhoi Su-24M strike aircraft, Su-34 multifunctional strike fighter aircraft, Su-25SM ground attack aircraft, Su-30SM multidimensional strike fighter aircraft, a number of helicopters used for air base defence and search and rescue operations and UAV for surveillance.

On the first day of combat operations eight separate target areas were struck by Su-24M, Su-34 and Su-25SM ground attack aircraft. Targets in the main consisted of ammunition storage, POL (Petroleum Oil Lubricants) storage, combat vehicles and command and communications posts. The following day the MODRF confirmed that a further four ISIS targets were struck "this night", suggesting that operations were conducted during the night of 30 September/1 October. It was confirmed that Su-24M strike aircraft and Su-25 ground attack aircraft had flown 8 sorties, the MODRF stating that "the staff of terrorist groupings and an ammunition depot near Idlib as well as a three-level HQ [Headquarters] centre near Hamah" were attacked. One of the strikes, it was stated by the MODRF, destroyed a facility used to prepare cars for attacks, presumably car bomb attacks. This latter facility was apparently located somewhere to the north of Homs.

A MODRF briefing held on 2 October stated that over the course of the previous 24 hours Su-24M strike aircraft and Su-25SM ground aircraft had flown 18 sorties, during which twelve ISIS targets, consisting of command & communications, bunkers, POL facilities and ammunition storage areas, had been engaged. It was stated that ten of these sorties were flown during the hours of darkness, striking seven of the targets over the course of the night of $1^{st}/2^{nd}$ October.

An ISIS HQ, described by the MODRF as a "fortified concrete object with equipped shelters" located close to the village of Kafr Zita in Hamah Province, was attacked by Su-24M strike aircraft. Post-strike OM (Objective Monitoring – damage assessment) footage indicated that a number of militarised vehicles, armed with large caliber machine guns, were destroyed, the figure indicated to be in excess of 24.

A further 14 strike sorties were flown from Hmeymim during daylight hours on 2 October, Su-24M and Su-25SM ground attack aircraft attacking what was described by the MODRF as a command centre located in the Hann Sayhun district of Idlib. Post-strike OM indicated that this target had been destroyed.

An MODRF briefing held on 3 October stated that Su-24M and Su-34 strike aircraft had flown 20 sorties, presumably the previous day, although it was indicated that at least some of these sorties may have been flown on the evening of the 2nd and or the night of 2/3 October. Nine separate targets were engaged, including what was described in the MODRF briefing as a "storage base for military hardware" in the Jisr al-Shughur district of Idlib, which was struck by Su-24M's. Further strikes in that district apparently destroyed an ammunition depot and other military equipment, including, as stated in the details of the briefing, a number of "all-terrain vehicles with large-caliber machine guns". It is though that this operation was attributed to the Su-24M detachment, although this has not been confirmed. Another strike by Su-24M's targeted an ammunition depot located in an uninhabited area of Syria's mountainous area near to Jisr al-Shughur, post-strike OM showing the target destroyed with a huge column of smoke rising from the target area.

On 4 October, the MODRF reported that over the course of the last day 20 strike sorties had been flown by Su-24M, Su-25SM and Su-34's, ten targets being engaged. Su-24M and Su-34's struck eight targets in the area of Jisr al-Shughur in the province of Idlib. This target grouping included three munitions storage facilities as well as POL facilities, which were apparently hit by KAB-500 guided bomb units launched from Su-24M's. Four targets, described by the MODRF as command posts, were destroyed by BETAB-500 concrete penetrating bombs, these, it is thought, attributed to Su-34 strikes.

Three sorties by Su-24M and Su-25SM (1 of one type and 2 of the other) were flown against an ammunition depot and a command post near the town of Maarat al Nu'man. Post-strike OM indicated that the targets had been destroyed.

On 5 October, the MODRF reported that over the course of the previous 24 hours there had been 25 strike sorties flown by Su-24M, Su-25SM and Su-34's, nine separate targets being struck. The sorties were apparently flown between late afternoon/evening of the 4th into the early morning of the 5th.

One daytime mission flown on the 4th consisted of a flight of two Su-24M's, which attacked a column of 32 vehicles close to Aleppo airfield which had been besieged by ISIS and affiliated forces for some time. By the end of the air attack most of the vehicles, many of which were equipped with ZU-23 23 mm anti-aircraft guns, were, according to the MODRF reports, destroyed.

Over the course of the night of 4/5 October, Su-24M's attacked what the MODRF described as an ISIS "rocket artillery" position located in a forest in the area of Jisr al-Shughur, Idlib. Post-strike OM showed the destruction of a MLRS (Multiple Launch Rocket System) and stored ammunition. Later briefings stated that some 30 vehicles, including light armored vehicles and tanks, had been destroyed.

A target, described in the MODRF briefing document as an "ISIS command centre" located in the vicinity of Al-Rastan in Homs, was destroyed in a strike by at least one Su-24M. Su-24M and Su-34's struck three targets at Talbiseh, Homs, two of these being described as ammunition storage depots. A target, described in the MODRF briefing document as a "communications centre" for coordinating opposition forces in the Homs district, was hit in a strike by Su-24M's. Post-strike OM showed that the building had been severely damaged. A target, described in the MODRF briefing document as an ISIS "command centre" at Bayt-Mnayna, Latakia, was struck by Su-24M's. Post-strike OM showed two fires at the location indicating severe damage or destruction of the facility.

Daytime operations on 5 October included 14 sorties by Su-24M, Su-25SM and Su-34's, during the course of which ten target areas were struck. In the area of Tadmor, to the east of Homs, a single Su-24M and a pair of Su-25SM's struck two separate target areas described by the MODRF as "concentrations of ISIS military hardware", which included up to twenty 1950/60's vintage T-55 Main Battle Tanks that had been seized from former Syrian Democratic Army facilities. The tanks were reported destroyed, their exploding fuel and ammunition causing a number of secondary fires in the surrounding area.

A Kh-25ML multi-purpose missile with a laser seeker head is loaded onto a Su-24M at Hmeymim air base. MODRF

An attack by one or more Su-24M strike aircraft was conducted against a target near to Tadmor, Homs, in which it was stated that three ISIS operated MLRS and an ammunition storage area were destroyed. It is unclear if this is related to the Su-24M strike in the Tadmor region previously mentioned for 5 October, or a separate operation.

Operations conducted during the day on 6 October included an undisclosed number of sorties by Su-24M, Su-25SM and Su-34's, during the course of which 12 targets were hit. These being stated by the MODRF to be "ISIS rear infrastructural facilities, command centres, training camps and militant bases". Su-24M's employed BETAB-500 concrete penetrating bombs against two ISIS command centers near Deir ez Zor, which had been besieged by significant ISIS forces since 2014.

Previous page and above: Su-24M's setting up for take-off and in the process of taking-off from Hmeymim air base in October 2015. White 04 (previous page top) is armed with OFAB-250/270 unguided high explosive bombs on the fuselage and wing stations and is configured with external fuel tanks on the shoulder wing stations. White 05 (previous page bottom and this page) are configured with fuselage and wing mounted OFAB-250/270 bombs. MODRF

In Idlib province, Su-24M's bombed what was described by the MODRF as an "ISIS terrorist training ground", strike camera footage showing several explosions within the target area.

A Su-24M strike, near to the Guta area of Damascus, was stated by the MODRF to have destroyed a plant used for the manufacture of explosive devices. The target was struck by KAB-500 variant guided bomb units.

In the early evening of 8 October, a MODRF briefing stated that 22 strikes sorties had been flown by Su-24M, Su-25SM and Su-34's that night, 27 separate targets being struck. It is unclear if those sorties were flown earlier on the 8th or perhaps the reference was intended for the previous night of the 7th/8th. During the course of these operations a force of Su-24M's and Su-34's struck a number of targets, stated by the MODRF to be eight, in the province of Homs. Post-strike assessments indicated that fortified positions were destroyed with a number of secondary explosions being observed, these apparently being the result of exploding munition and fuel storages.

Contrary to the mass media reporting of indiscriminate bombing that circulated in the western press, Russia aircraft often returned with their ordnance as shown by White 04 landing at Hmeymim with its bombs (previous page) if targets could not be verified or engaged with a reasonable degree of confidence in regards to accuracy. Above: A typical ordnance load for an Su-24M mission would consist of 4 x OFAB-250/270 high explosive blast fragmentation bombs as seen on White 26. MODRF

The MODRF briefing document dated 9 October stated that over the previous 24 hours Su-24M, Su-34 and Su-25SM strike/attack aircraft had flown 67 operational sorties, during the course of which some 60 targets had been engaged in the provinces of Aleppo, Idlib, Raqqah, Lattakia and Hamah. The sum of these strikes, as stated in the briefing document, was the destruction of "6 command and communications centres; 6 ammunition and POL depots; 17 training camps of terrorists; 3 underground facilities of militants in the Lattakia province; 16 fortified areas and defensive positions with armament and military hardware; 11 concentration areas for reserves of the illegal armed groups; a plant for repairing of armoured vehicles; 17 automobile and armoured vehicles; 2 MLRS systems."

The MODRF briefing document dated 10 October stated that over the previous 24 hours the Aerospace Group Su-24M, Su-34 and Su-25SM strike/attack aircraft had flown 64 sorties, during the course of which 55 targets had been engaged in the provinces of Aleppo, Raqqah, Hamah and Damascus. As detailed in the briefing document, targets consisted of "2 command centres; an ammunition depot in Hamah province; 29 field camps of terrorists; 23 fortified areas and strong points…"

The increase in the tempo of air operations over the previous two days or so was due to the detection of increased numbers of targets on the ground by reconnaissance assets. Significant among the claims made by MODRF was the destruction of what it described as the "main and largest ISIS logistic centres"; targeting of such centres being instrumental in reducing the available resources of stores, such as ammunition and POL, available to militants on the ground. This, it was stated by the MODRF, being confirmed by interception of radio signals. The resultant shortages apparently had the net effect of causing whole units to abandon their positions opposite Syrian government forces. These militant units then moved to other areas in the East and North-East of Syria.

Specific missions conducted by the Su-24M detachment included an attack on a fortified position that included fire positions and emplacements for mortars/artillery, which was located to the east of Tel-Alam in Aleppo province. This position was destroyed by a flight of Su-24M strike aircraft employing BETAB-500 concrete penetrating bombs. An opposition forces base area near the settlement of Kuweires in Aleppo province was attacked by a Su-24M strike aircraft. Post-strike imagery showed that around ten vehicles were destroyed, which included 5 IFV (Infantry Fighting Vehicles) and 2 tanks.

The MODRF briefing document dated 11 October stated that over the previous 24 hours the Aerospace Group Su-24M, Su-34 and Su-25SM strike/attack aircraft had flown 64 sorties, during the course of which 63 targets had been engaged in the provinces of Idlib, Raqqah, Hamah and Lattakia. As detailed in the briefing document, targets included "53 fortified areas and strong points... 2 command centres; 4 field camps... 7 ammunition depots; artillery and mortar batteries."

Specific Su-24M operations included a mission in which an Su-24M bombed a target, described in the MODRF briefing document as an "ISIS coordinating centre" that was apparently used for coordination of ground forces. Post-strike OM showed that this target, which was located in the area of Salma in Latakia, had been destroyed by a direct hit registered by a KAB-500 variant guided bomb unit. In addition to the main target, five-off road vehicles, armed with ZU-23 AA guns, were also destroyed.

A concealed position housing a mobile mortar battery, consisting of a number of off-road vehicles armed with mortar tubes, was located in the area of Kafr Delba in Lattakia province. A Su-24M attacked with the result that the battery, including no less than six vehicles, was destroyed.

The MODRF briefing document dated 12 October stated that over the previous 24 hours the Aerospace Group Su-24M, Su-34 and Su-25SM strike/attack aircraft had flown 55 sorties, during the course of which 53 targets had been engaged in the provinces of Homs, Hamah, Lattakia and Idlib. As detailed in the briefing document, targets included "25 fortified areas and defensive positions... a terrorist strong point near Salam settlement (Lattakia Province); 7 command centres... 6 terrorist field training camps; 6 ammunition depots; a column of automobile vehicles; 3 underground shelters in the Lattakia province; 1 mobile mortar group."

Specific Su-24M operations detailed in the 12 October briefing document included an attack on an ISIS underground facility incorporating a munitions depot near the settlement of Salma in Lattakia Province, which had been detected by space based surveillance assets. This target was then attacked by Su-24M's employing fragmentation bombs. Post-strike OM showed that the target had been destroyed by detonation of the stored munitions. Su-24M activity over Hamah province included an attack on an ISIS underground command centre, which was destroyed by a KAB-500 variant guide bomb unit.

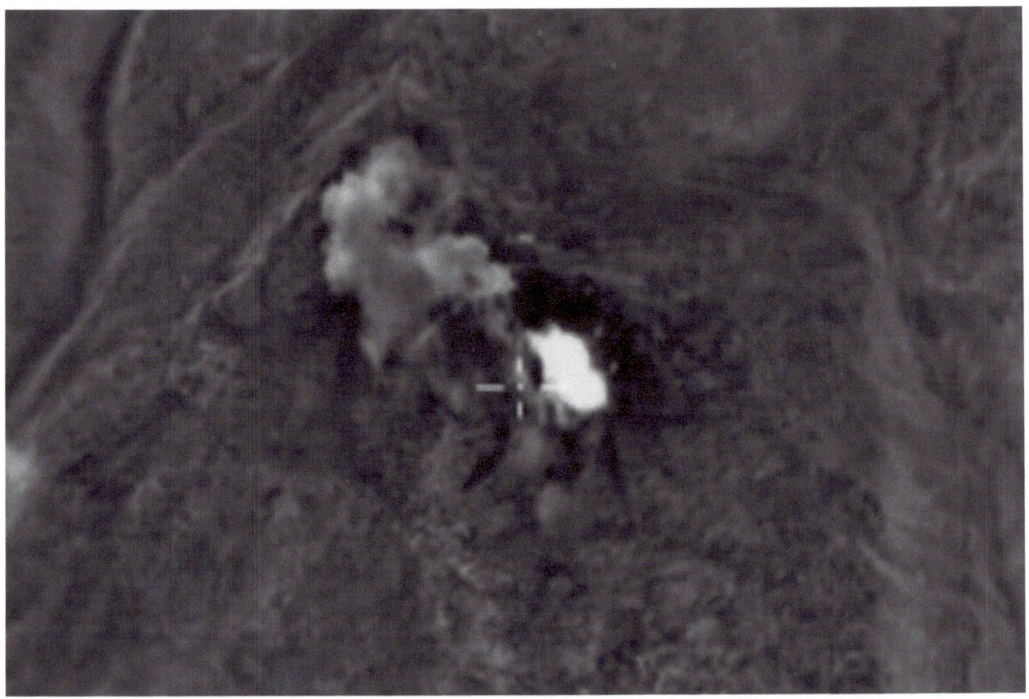

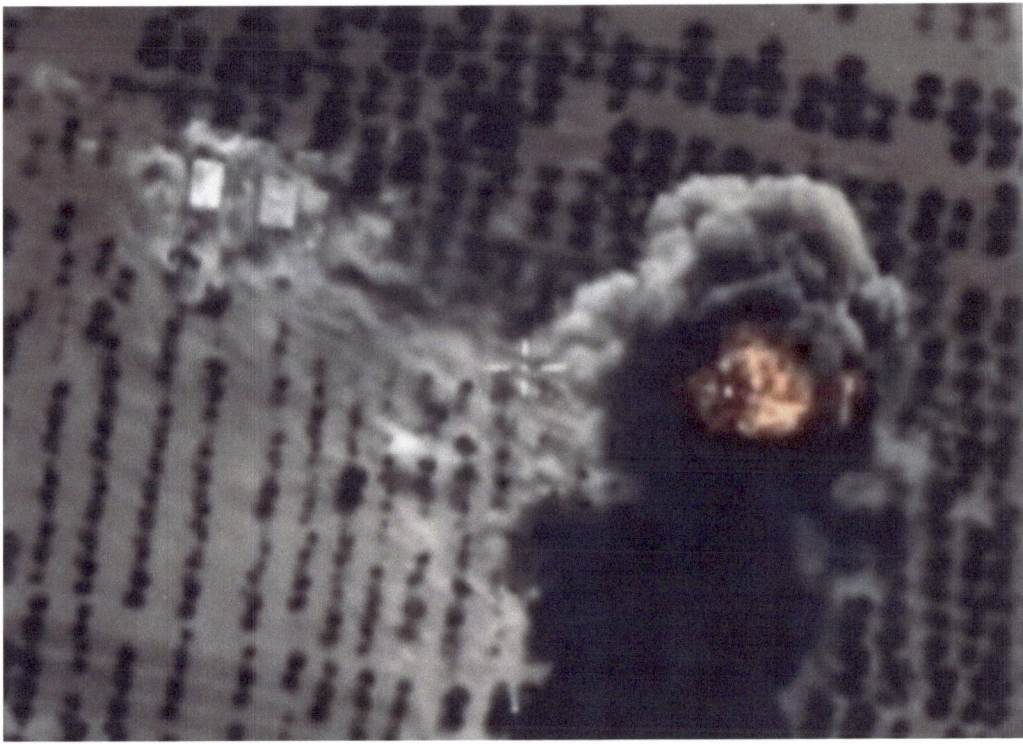

Top: An ISIS underground facility in wooded/mountainous terrain near Salam in Lattakia Province is struck by ordnance from an Su-24M. Above: A precision guided strike by a Su-24M on opposition forces armored vehicles concealed in a fertile area of Idlib Province. MODRF

The MODRF briefing document dated 14 October stated that over the previous 24 hours the Aerospace Group Su-24M, Su-34 and Su-25SM strike/attack aircraft had flown 41 operational sorties, during the course of which 40 targets had been engaged in the provinces of Aleppo, Idlib, Lattakia, Hama and Deir ez-Zor. Specific Su-24M operations included an attack on a facility near Aleppo, stated by the MODRF to be active in the manufacture of explosive devices and the installation of same on vehicles for use by suicide bombers.

Munitions depots in Hama and Lattakia provinces were destroyed by ordnance released by Su-24M strike aircraft and Su-24M's were also active over Deir ez-Zor, an ISIS command centre being destroyed in the latter province. Another strike, about 13 miles south of Aleppo, destroyed a facility apparently used to repair armoured vehicles and convert off-road vehicles to carry weapons such as mortars, large calibre machine guns and ZU-23 23 mm AA guns. The type of aircraft that conducted this strike was not stated in the briefing document, but is assumed to have been either Su-24M or Su-34 strike aircraft.

The MODRF briefing document dated 15 October showed a decrease in the tempo of air operations over the previous 24 hours, with 33 operational sorties being flown by Su-24M, Su-34 and Su-25SM strike/attack aircraft, during the course of which 32 targets had been engaged in the provinces of Aleppo, Idlib, Hama, Damascus and Deir ez-Zor. The decrease in operational tempo was attributed to uncertainty in targeting as ISIS conducted large scale withdrawals from areas under the weight of the air offensive, which was supporting advances by Syrian Democratic Army forces on the ground. While the tempo of strike operations decreased, the tempo of reconnaissance flights by aircraft and UAV increased in an effort to gather information on new positions being taken up by opposition ground forces.

Specific Su-24M operations flown during the above detailed period included an attack on an ISIS command centre located in a two-story building in Aleppo Province. This target was destroyed by a bomb released from a Su-24M. Su-24M's attacked shelters housing what was described by the MODRF as "armoured hardware" as well as POL and other material storage facilities in Idlib Province.

At an MODRF briefing on 16 October 2015, the Chief of the Main Operational Directorate of the General Staff of the Russian Armed Forces, Colonel Andrei Kartapolov, stated that the Russian Aerospace Group had, over the course of the previous week, "destroyed 46 command centres and 6 plants of the ISIS." Through the period in question the Aerospace Group had flown 394 combat sorties. Targets struck included 22 POL facilities along with 272 other targets, consisting of opposition forces troop concentrations, fortified positions and a number of training facilities.

By 16 October 2015, the total number of combat sorties flown by the Russian Aerospace Group since the commencement of the operation on 30 September stood at 699, which included 115 nighttime sorties (it is unclear if these values include air defence sorties or refer only to strike/attack sorties). The post targeting apparatus had, according to the MODRF, shown that "456 objects had been destroyed".

The 17 October MORDF briefing stated that on the 16th strikes were conducted on "command centres, workshops manufacturing munitions as well as firing artillery positions, depots with armament, ammunition and reserves of military equipment of the ISIS terrorist organisation." The days operations had involved 36 combat sorties, during the course of which 49 targets were struck in the provinces of Hama, Idlib, Damascus and Aleppo resulting in, as stated by MODRF furnished data, the destruction of "11 command and control centres... a plant manufacturing improvised explosive devices; 3 firing artillery positions... 2 bases of combat vehicles; 15 field camps and terrorist bases; 8 fortified and defensive positions."

Specific targets attacked by the Su-24M detachment included a large building near to Salam in Latakia Province that intelligence data had identified as, as stated by the MODRF, a facility where "foreign instructors prepared ISIS militants for sabotage war against the districts liberated by the Syrian Army, as well as suicide bombers". The building, continued the MODRF statement, "also contained a workshop for production of improvised explosive devices. The building was attacked by a Su-24M which destroyed the facility with one or more direct bomb hits of undisclosed ordnance type.

Another Su-24M strike was directed at targets in the suburbs of Damascus, described by the MODRF as "two ammunition depots and a workshop manufacturing improvised explosive devices for the ISIS terrorists". The targets were completely destroyed in what the MODRF described as "precision strikes". In the area of Marj al-Sultan a Su-24M targeted a command centre, stated by the MODRF as belonging to the Faylak Omar group, which intelligence had apparently confirmed was responsible for a number of terrorist attacks in government held areas of Homs and Damascus Provinces. The direct hit by one or more bombs completely destroyed the building housing the alleged command centre.

The MODRF briefing document dated 18 October stated that over the previous 24 hours Russian aircraft had flown 39 operational sorties, during the course of which 60 separate strikes had been conducted against 51 targets in the provinces of Aleppo, Hama, Lattakia and Damascus. These operations had, as stated in the briefing document, eliminated "4 command centres... 6 ammunition and armament depots; a mortar battery; 2 underground bunkers; 32 field camps of terrorists; 6 strong points."

Specific operations flown by the Su-24M detachment included the targeting of what was referred to in the MODRF briefing document as an "ISIS ammunition storage hidden in mountainous area". This target was destroyed by one or more weapons released by the Su-24M. Su-24M's also struck a target described in the MODRF briefing document as a command centre in the suburbs of north western Kafr Zita in Hama Province. Post-strike OM indicated that this facility, which was apparently used by the Jaysh Al-Fetah group, was destroyed. This attack, along with other offensive pressure, caused disruption in the command and control of the group, leading to withdrawal of a number of units from the combat line facing the Syrian Democratic Army. Withdrawals of opposition units continued in many parts of East and North-East Syria under air and ground offensive pressure. In addition, many of the opposition groups were at odds with each other over whom controlled assets and money in the various regions, leading to attacks by one group against another, the favoured tactic being the detonation of car bombs at command centres.

Page 52: Su-24M's landing at Hmeymim air base. This page: An Su-24M lands at Hmeymim (top) and an Su-25SM lands (bottom). MODRF

The MODRF briefing document dated 19 October stated that over the previous 24 hours Russian aircraft had flown 33 operational sorties, during the course of which 49 targets were engaged in the provinces of Aleppo, Hama, Lattakia, Idlib and Damascus. Specific targets sets stated to have been eliminated included "2 command centres of illegal armed groups; 3 depots with ammunition and armament; 2 underground bunkers; 32 firing positions in mountain-woody areas; 9 fortified firing positions… and a workshop used for production of launching ramps and rocket projectiles".

An air reconnaissance by UAV near Al-Ess in Idlib Province detected what was determined to be a command centre belonging to units of the Jabhat al-Nusra group. Further intelligence assets were focused on the area, which confirmed the target as a command centre. An Su-24M was tasked to strike the target with at least one bomb leading to the destruction of the building housing the command centre and the destruction of 2 trucks armed with ZU-23 23 mm AA guns that were located next to the building.

Attacks by Russian aircraft, described by the MODRF as precision strikes, were conducted in Damascus Province, contributing significantly to the changing operational situation on the ground in favour of the Syrian Democratic Army units, with significant numbers of opposition forces abandoning their prepared positions. Several units, of about 100 or so persons each, being noted withdrawing in the direction of Marj al-Sultan.

The MODRF briefing document dated 20 October stated that over the previous 24 hours Russian aircraft had flown 55 operational sorties, during the course of which 60 targets, predominantly associated with ISIS or Jabhat al-Nusra groups, were engaged in the provinces of Aleppo, Hama, Lattakia, Idlib, Damascus and Deir ez-Zor. Specific targets sets, stated in the briefing document as having been destroyed, included "19 command centres… 2 depots with ammunition; a plant used for production of munitions and explosives; 30 firing positions and concentrations of military hardware; underground fortified facilities". Specific targets attacked by the Su-24M detachment included a concealed ammunition depot and a command centre in the area of Qastun, Idlib Province. Post-strike OM indicated that this target had been destroyed, the munitions launched from the Su-24M (type undisclosed) touching-off stored munitions resulting in a number of large explosions that ripped through the target area.

The MODRF briefing document dated 21 October stated that over the previous 24 hours Russian aircraft had flown 46 operational sorties, during the course of which 83 targets were engaged in the provinces of Aleppo, Hama, Idlib, Damascus and Deir ez-Zor.

Russian UAV surveillance assets identified a command-surveillance centre on Seryatel Mountain in Idlib Province. This system, deemed by the MODRF to belong to ISIS, was stated to be of the type that could allow the adjustment of aim of mortar firing as well as providing additional command and control functions over ground forces in contact with an opposing force, making it a priority target. The Aerospace Group allocated a Su-24M to strike the target (ordnance type undisclosed). Su-24M's were also active in other areas of Syria, one such aircraft attacking a target described by the MODRF as a concealed ISIS munitions depot in the area of Jisr al-Shughur in Idlib Province. The target was destroyed by undisclosed ordnance type launched from at least one Su-24M.

Su-24M's at Hmeymim air base, Syria. MODRF.

The MODRF briefing document dated 22 October stated that over the previous 24 hours Su-24M, Su-34 and Su-25SM strike/attack aircraft had flown 53 operational sorties, during the course of which 72 targets were engaged in the provinces of Aleppo, Hama, Idlib, Lattakia, Damascus and Deir ez-Zor. At this stage in the Russian campaign the MODRF acknowledged a change in tactics in that early in the campaign strike/attack aircraft mainly operated in pairs, but, as stated in the briefing document, recently, "due to good knowledge of the combat area the aircraft eliminate two or more targets individually in the course of one sortie". This was apparently one of the reasons behind the decreased sortie rate of the Aerospace Group, contradicting the unfounded Pentagon claim of the time that the decrease was due to a lack of targets.

A further briefing held on 22 October addressed the Aerospace Groups operations over the previous week. It was clarified that the main focus of the Russian operation concerned providing battlefield air support for the Syrian Democratic Army units engaged in operations to retake towns and villages that had been occupied by ISIS and Jabhat an-Nusra forces as well as other opposition groups, although the briefing specifically mentioned only the two former groups. MODRF intelligence confirmed that ISIS losses in Syria had led to the transfer of forces from Northern Iraq to bolster ISIS in Syria.

The total sortie count for the week stood at 934, in which, it was stated in the document, 819 "facilities" were deemed to have been destroyed. Contradicting this statement, the same briefing provided details that 363 targets had been destroyed over the past week, these including "71 command centres, 10 plants and workshops manufacturing explosives, 30 different POL, material and ammunition depots, 252 fortified areas, strong points and field camps of terrorists". This of course may simply have been a mix up in wording that possibly failed to take into account some of the operations in support of the Syrian Democratic Army.

It was becoming clear at this stage of the campaign that the attacks by Su-24M strike aircraft were typically conducted from altitudes in the region of 6000 m, somewhat higher than the 5000 m altitude that the majority of Su-34 attacks were being conducted from.

4

SDA GROUND OFFENSIVES – OCTOBER 2015-MARCH 2016

Whilst the Syrian conflict is an ongoing tragedy even as these words are written in early 2017, this volume covers only the Russian supported ground operations up to mid-March 2016, which could be considered the end of the first phase of the Russian campaign in Syria that led to a shaky ceasefire that ultimately crumbled as fighting continued throughout Syria. This phase is considered to have ended with the first liberation of the ancient historic site of Palmyra from ISIS (Islamic State of Iraq and the Levant) occupation in March 2016 (Palmyra was recaptured by ISIS in late 2016 in an ISIS offensive designed to draw-off Syrian government and Russian forces from the offensive against Jabhat al Nusra and other opposition forces in Aleppo. Palmyra was subsequently recaptured in early March 2017 after the fall of Aleppo).

It would be an understatement to state that by late summer 2015 the Syrian conflict that had begun with internal unrest in 2011, was a quagmire of internal groups and no little external interference as various factions and power blocks maneuvered for an outcome favorable to each. In this regard, the so called 'moderate opposition', feeling let down by the western powers whom they viewed as having encouraged an uprising that led to civil war, had, to all intents and purposes become pawns of regional powers such as Saudi Arabia, backed by western powers, in a wider game that was drawing in ever more external players. The end result of Saudi and western powers financial and military support for such groups was the facilitation of ISIS entrenchment in Syria as the growth of ISIS in Syria stemmed from the inability of the Syrian armed forces to adequately combat the movement as it was bogged down fighting the so called 'moderate opposition' groups.

A fair assessment of the situation on the ground in summer 2015 would be that the Syrian Government forces were in many areas on the verge of collapse under the threefold campaigns of the so called 'moderate opposition' forces, ISIS and affiliates and the ever increasing threat of attack, indeed, invasion, by the western powers and further destabilizing interference by regional powers such as Saudi Arabia. Indeed, it was the threat of air attack on Syrian government held areas by western powers and an ad-hoc invasion force sponsored by and possibly including Saudi forces that prompted Russia to respond to a call for assistance by the Syrian Arab Republic government by deploying naval, air and a limited base protection ground force element to Syria in late summer 2015. The Russian mandate was clear – support the Syrian government forces in their defensive and offensive battles against ISIS and other groups deemed as terrorist organisations. In reality this would encompass much of the so called 'moderate opposition' groups that were fighting against SDA (Syrian Democratic Army) forces, thereby supporting the overall external and internal threats to Syria's territorial integrity.

The indisputable success of the Russian air campaign in Syria in comparison to the abject failure of the self-styled 'anti-ISIS' coalition air campaign stemmed from the fact that the Russian campaign was operating in direct support of a credible ground force capable of capitalising on the air support provided and go on the offensive. The success of the campaign was evident in the defeat of ISIS and other opposition groups leading to large swathes of territory being brought back under Syrian Government control.

By the middle of October 2015, it had become clear that there was a clearly definable method in the way the Russian air campaign was being conducted. The major part of the air effort was being flown in support of SDA ground forces. On 16 October, the Russian Federation General Staff stated emphatically that the Russian air attacks had caused serious disruption in opposition ground forces including, as stated by Chief of the Main Operational Directorate of the General Staff of the Russian Armed Forces, Andrei Kartapolov, "infrastructure, supply and control systems". This had caused a sea shift in the situation on the ground, which, prior to the Russian intervention, had been dire for the SDA, which was overstretched in its battle against ISIS and the so called 'moderate' opposition forces. The situation was so severe that SDA units were being overwhelmed in many areas, particularly by ISIS, which had proven to be a far more formidable fighting organisation than the 'moderate' opposition forces, which, despite being supported by the self-styled 'anti-ISIS' coalition, was riddled by infighting as various groups vied for territorial control.

By mid-October, the situation on the ground had improved to the point where the SDA, with the support provided by the Russian Aerospace Group, was more able to effectively counter the multitude of groups facing them. Kartapolov stated that intelligence data gleaned from air reconnaissance and intercepted radio transmissions showed that "every night up to 100 armed extremists of Jabhat al-Nusra cross the [Turkish] border near Reyhani, and ISIS terrorists cross the border near Jarabulus." Such intelligence data clearly showed that, while it was suffering setbacks on the battlefield, ISIS and its affiliates were still able to call on a steady stream of reinforcements and supplies from outside Syria. While reinforcements of personnel were proving very difficult to counter as extremists continued to cross from Syria's porous borders, particularly from Iraq and Turkey, it was clear that significant numbers of heavy weapons on the contact line with the SDA had been destroyed or abandoned as opposition forces withdrew.

During the course of the week ending on 22 October 2015, a major focus of SDA ground operations was in the suburbs of southern Aleppo, where the 'Sheikh Ahmed' group was claimed by the MODRF to have been "completely liquidated".

MODRF intelligence also stated that in Aleppo, so called "retreat-blocking detachments" had been formed by opposition forces with the specific aim of preventing untrained militants from withdrawing from their positions. Such statements, of course, prove to be more or less impossible to have independent verification of, although in the battle for Aleppo in late 2016 such detachments were very active in preventing civilians leaving opposition held areas for government held areas, a situation, while more or less ignored by much of the western media, was detailed by those fortunate to make the crossing under fire and live streaming webcams on the various crossing points.

It was clear towards the end of October 2015, that the support provided by the Russian aviation assets had facilitated a considerable change in the situation on the ground as the SDA was retaking ground previously occupied by one opposition group or another. This led to the first serious overtures for negotiations by opposition groups previously emboldened by the capturing of territory from Syrian government forces. For the first time too, it was becoming clear to the western powers and their Middle East allies that they were backing, and had become actively involved in a conflict, in which they had made demands on the Syrian government that they were no longer in a position to militarily enforce.

At this time the SDA main efforts were being directed at stabilising and or regaining lost territory in the provinces of Aleppo, Latakia, Idlib, Homs and Damascus. In Aleppo, Jdeideh falling to government forces on 21 October and SDA units continued to push forward in the direction of Kuweires airbase. To the southeast of Aleppo, the settlements of Sabikia, Khan Tuman, Harasi, Khan al-Assal, and Shughaydilah had been retaken and SDA units were preparing to launch an assault on opposition forces entrenched in the settlement of Balas. It was in the operation to retake Khan Tuman that reports emerged, reiterated in MODRF operational briefings, that civilians were used as human shields by opposition forces (the author has not been able to have these reports independently verified at the time of publication). Fighting continued in North-West Aleppo as SDA units slowly retook areas previously occupied by opposition forces with the intention of cutting them off from opposition forces operating outside the city.

The main focus of ground operations in Latakia Province was aimed at probing for weak points in the militant's defensive positions and the active engagement of militant positions that were firing into areas under government control. In this general area SDA units had cut off and were preparing to move against opposition forces in the settlements of Salma and Simania.

SDA operations in central Syria resulted in the capture of the outskirts of Teyr Maala and barrier operations were conducted against opposition forces in Dar al Kaveer. Other operations in the central areas were directed at suppressing or destroying enemy fire positions. There was clear evidence that many opposition groups, ISIS and others, were encountering an increased rate of desertion from the ranks, mainly to regions in the rear of the immediate combat zones, but also across Syria's borders with her neighbors. In the latter regard MODRF statements specifically mentioned Turkey and Jordan as being particular havens for what it deemed to be terrorists.

During the last week of October it had become clear that the Russian campaign of military intervention had dramatically altered the strategic situation on the ground, having caused major disruption and losses among opposition fielded forces, command and control, including, as stated in MODRF briefing documentation, the "elimination" of a number of "odious terrorist" leaders, and logistics organisations. The SDA, which had previously been forced onto the defensive, was able to take the offensive against such groups as ISIS and Jabhat al-Nusra as well as elements of the so-called 'moderate' opposition.

Intelligence data, it was stated by the MODRF, showed that reinforcements for areas such as Aleppo increasingly continued to be drawn from ISIS forces in Northern Iraq. The beginning of closer ties between the so called 'moderate' opposition and more extremist groups commenced with the apparent linking of the Jabhat al-Nusra and Harakat Ahrar ash-Sham groups, the latter supported by the anti-ISIS coalition and the former having affiliations with al-Qaida, giving currency to the Syrian government and Russian view that there was little that separated the groups in their military ambitions and ideologically. This view was further reinforced as other elements of Jabhat al-Nusra located in Hama Province forged closer links with ISIS as both faced an offensive by the SDA.

SDA offensive operations were conducted in the provinces of Aleppo, Latakia, Idlib, Homs and Damascus, leading to the removal of opposition control over some 350 sq. km of territory encompassing more than 50 towns and villages, 19 of which were near to Aleppo. Most of these gains had been achieved during the SDA defensive and counter offensive operations against opposition forces intent on expanding the territory under their control. The SDA also redoubled their efforts to secure Kuweires air base in Aleppo Province.

SDA operations in Latakia Province forced opposition forces to abandon 9 settlements, while operations in Hama Province in central Syria led to opposition forces being forced away from 12 towns. An SDA offensive in Homs Province, supported by loyal militia forces, led to the capture of the town of Sanasil and facilitated the encirclement of opposition forces in a number of areas, including Al-Dar al-Kabirah, Deir-Semali, and Teir Maalah. SDA operations were also directed against opposition forces in Damascus, in particular the Eastern Guta district and near to Douma and Nulah where a number of successes were noted. SDA advances in the direction of Jobar were aimed at encircling opposition forces in that general area.

By 11 November, SDA operations, supported by Russian air strikes, had removed the opposition forces blockade of Kuweires air base in Aleppo Province, lifting a two year siege. SDA forces also moved against what was stated as 7 separate opposition units with a combined strength of some 900 personnel located near the settlements of Azizyah, Kafer Haddad and Tel Mano. The ground operations, combined with air operations that interdicted supplies, led to the destruction of the units as organised fighting forces, the remnants withdrawing from the area.

During the period 23-26 November 2015, the continued heavy losses by opposition forces due to Russian airstrikes led to the ceding of territory as rebel forces withdrew 4-6 km back towards Mahin, Al-Qaratayn.

Certainly in the first week or so of December 2015, the area in which an Su-24M pilot had been killed by opposition forces as he descended from strike aircraft which crashed after being struck by an AIM-9 Sidewinder infrared guided air to air missile launched form a Turkish F-16 fighter aircraft on 24 November 2015, was brought under government control with a comprehensive defeat for opposition forces on the ground. Many of the militants then abandoned the fight and fled across the Turkish border in the face of the SDA advances by what was termed a 'Special Task Force'. The offensive operation enabled the Su-24M wreckage to be located and the black box recovered and returned to Russia.

Into the second week of December 2015, SDA ground operations, under the support of Russian and Syrian aircraft, continued at a steady pace with several offensive operations taking place in the provinces of Latakia, Aleppo and Homs. In addition, offensive operations continued in the suburbs of Damascus whilst defensive operations continued in many other areas of Syria, including the SDA Eastern bastion in Deir ez-Zor.

The SDA offensive operations in Aleppo Province were aimed mainly at continuing the expansion of the so called security zone around Kuweires air base and the continuation of offensive operations pushing south-westward in the direction of Idlib. These operations had led to the removal of opposition forces from a number of inhabited areas, nine of which had been captured by SDA units over the previous week or so.

Offensive operations in Latakia Province were aimed at opposition forces in the Northern and Western areas. In the North of Latakia, SDA units increased the area under their control on the Syria-Turkish border. The increasing pressure being exerted on opposition forces led to their abandoning strategically important high ground near to Simaniyah and Salma.

SDA offensive operations in central Syria resulted in setbacks for opposition forces, which included the capture of a number of strategically important high ground locations in the area of Mahin. SDA offensive operations in the suburbs of Damascus were mainly in the shape of small scale offensives that reduced the area under opposition forces control. These operations were specifically in the directions of al-Sultan, an-Nula, Duma and Zibdin.

The SDA operations were, indirectly, supported by what were in effect opposition units numbering some 5,000 personnel that were responding to the severe threat that ISIS posed to the entirety of Syria. However, the majority of the so called 'moderate' opposition forces continued to operate mainly against the Syrian government forces, a situation that, as previously noted, had allowed ISIS to gain such a strong foothold in Syria. A varying percentage of Russian air strikes had been conducted in direct support of opposition units operating against ISIS, 17 having been conducted, apparently in support of the 'Ganim' detachment of the self-styled 'FSA' ('Free Syrian Army') to the North of Raqqah on 14/15 December alone. According to the MODRF, these particular strikes resulted in an ISIS loss of 11 personnel and 11 pieces of hardware (undetermined). A further 18 air strikes had been conducted on ISIS positions in support of the 'Desert Lions' and 'Kalamun' groupings near to Palmyra and El-Karatien.

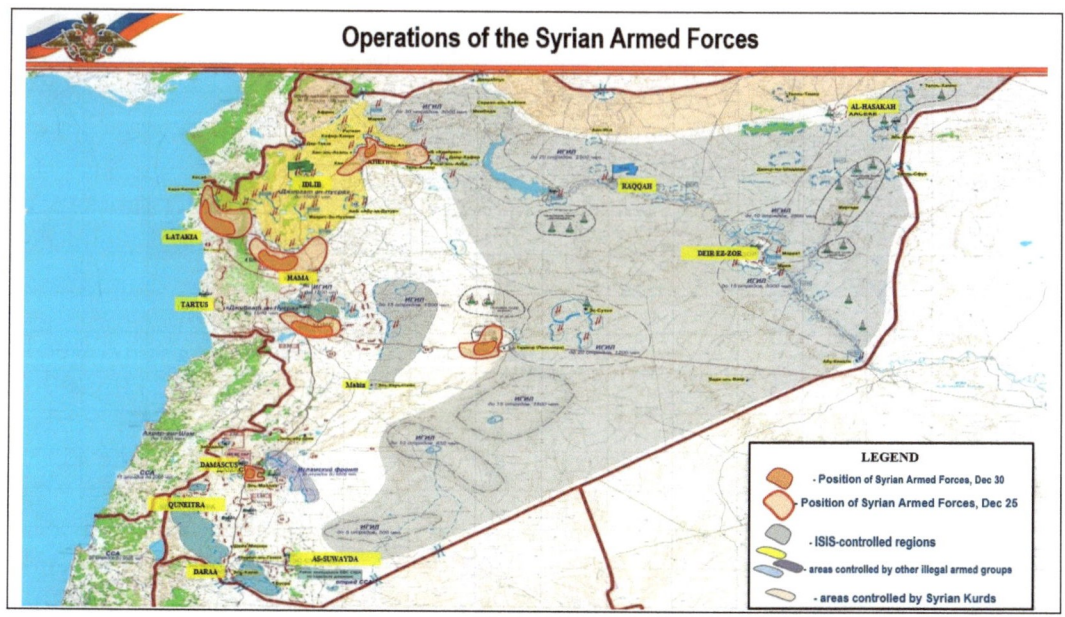

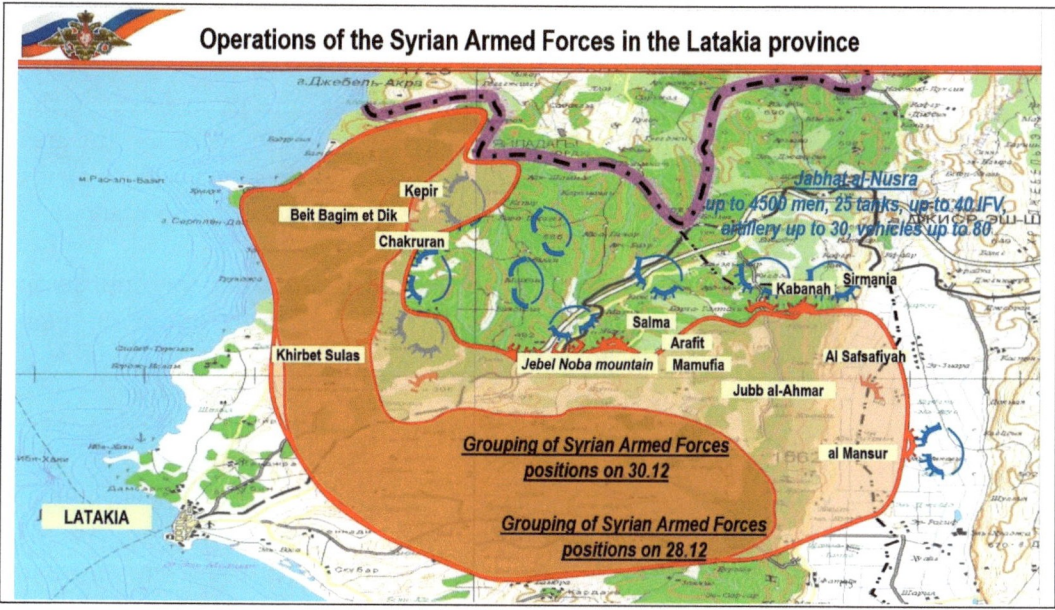

Top: Map of the Syrian Arab Republic indicating the areas controlled by Syrian Government Forces and the major opposition groups, including ISIS, in the last week of December 2015. MODRF Above: Map showing the areas of major operations of the Syrian Armed Forces in Latakia Province of Syria in the last week of December 2015. MODRF

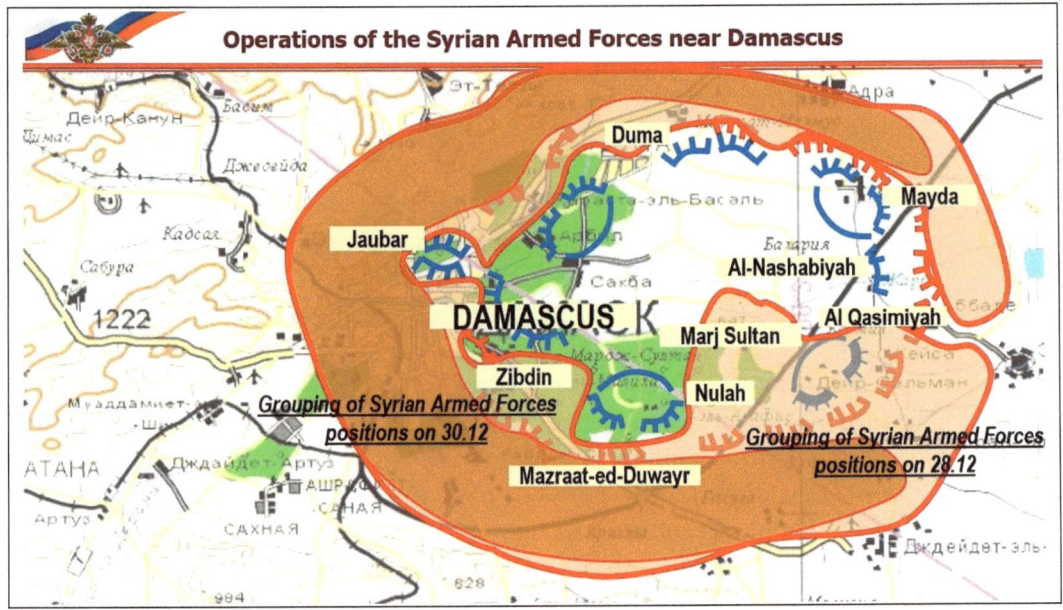

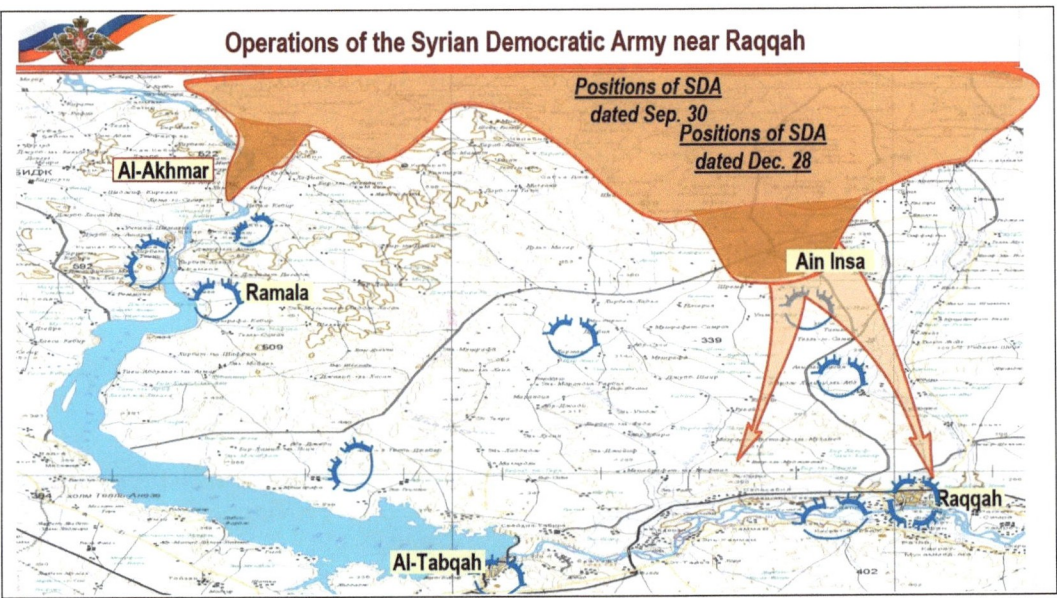

Top: Map showing the areas of operations of the Syrian Armed Forces near Damascus in the last week of December 2015. MODRF

Above: Map showing the areas of operations of the Syrian Democratic Army near Raqqah in the last week of December 2015. MODRF

In the second half of December 2015, much of the Russian effort was directed at supporting offensive operations by SDA units in a number of areas, the most successful ground operations taking place in the suburbs of Damascus and in Latakia Province. The offensive operations in Damascus led to the capture of the settlement of Marj al-Sultan as SDA units continued their push towards Nahsabia, Nula, Duma and Zibdin, in the drive to encircle opposition forces. SDA forces had also continued their advance in the area of Eastern Guta.

In Latakia Province, SDA units continued to advance in northerly and easterly directions. In this regard SDA units occupied the area of the left bank of the Kebir River, covering the Turkish-Syrian border to the settlement of Soraf. Three points of high ground were occupied by SDA units moving in the direction of Kabanah and Simaniayh. Continuation of SDA offensive operations pushed North and East in Latakia Province, tactically important high ground and the settlement of Kepir being captured (conflicting information emanating from the MODRF suggests that this may have been defensive battles to hold-off opposition forces attacks) as the offensive pushed in the direction of Kobani and Simania. What is clear is that the Jebel Noba height was captured by SDA units.

The major operation in Aleppo Province was the continuing expansion of territory under SDA control around the Kuweires air base. Among the main results was the recapture of 5 settlements. To the North of Kuweires air base several settlements and the Tell Sherbae heights were captured. In Raqqah Province, offensive operations continued against the de facto ISIS capital, Raqqah. SDA units captured the dam over the river Euphrates Near al-Akmar. Defensive, stabilising and minor offensive operations continued in other areas of Syria.

The support provided by Russian airpower had enabled the SDA to continue its offensive operations despite the onset of winter weather. Going into the second week of January the situation on the ground had deteriorated significantly for the opposition forces that had been driven out of no less than 134 towns and settlements during the course of December 2015 and a further 19 towns and settlements were brought under government control during the first ten days of 2016 as opposition forces continued to withdraw.

The most notable success's for the SDA were in the provinces of Aleppo, Latakia, Hama, Homs and Raqqah. SDA operations in Aleppo Province continued to be focused mainly on enhancing the security zone established around Kuweires airbase, this resulting in a northward advance of around 5 km over the few days leading up to 11 January. Further operations resulted in the removal of opposition forces from the town of Naijara and the settlement of Ayishah. In operations in the South-West of Aleppo Province, SDA forces pushed opposition forces out of the towns of Abu Ruwayl and Hawbar.

SDA forces continued offensive operations in Latakia Province, pushing northward and eastward. A number of high ground locations were captured as were several inhabited areas, notably Mughayriyah and Kadin, both deemed important areas in the development of future operations. The opposition groups, which were suffering significant material and personnel losses, continued to be reinforced regularly from across the Turkish border with the Northern tip of Latakia Province.

In Hama Province, SDA forces advanced some 12-15 km in a south-easterly direction forcing opposition forces to abandon the towns of Jarniyah, Ramila and Jarjisah. The city of Mahin in Homs Province was liberated by SDA forces which had advanced in an Eastern direction towards the city of Al-Qaryatayn. Operations in Damascus were focused on several battles that raged close to Eastern Guta as SDA forces advanced in the direction of Blaila, Nashabiiyah and Haush Jarabo with the intention of pushing opposition forces out of these locations. In Daraa Province, SDA units advanced into the city of Shaykh Maskin, which was, by 11 January, stated to be mostly under the control of government forces.

At this time it was noted that the Russian Aerospace Group had continued to fly sorties in support of some opposition groups fighting the common enemy. The MODRF then understood the strength of such groups to be around 7,000 personnel. Specifically, it was noted that over the previous several days 19 sorties had been flown in direct support of the 'Djeish Ahrar al-Ashaeir' group (apparently originating as the Southern front of the so called 'Free Syrian Army'). Air support was provided as the group was at that time opposing the extremist groups in the area of Taffa, as well as conducting blocking operations against extremist groups in Daraa Province.

In Raqqah Province the SDA continued offensive operations towards the city of Raqqah. A number of towns and settlements, al-Salkhiya, Rdjeman, Alya, al-Kria and Khadriyat Ayn Issa were recaptured. Operations by the 'Soureign' and 'Chelobiya' units continued to push opposition forces back as they expanded the area under their control on the Eastern and Western sides of the Euphrates Dam near to Mahshiyat al-Tawahin, Jubb Hamzah, Arba's Seighir, al-Jdeigeh and al-Akhmar.

The groups 'Lions of the East' and 'Kalumun', fighting against ISIS, advanced in excess of 50 km and captured the towns and settlements of Zara, Kessara and el-Mhasse. This operation was an element of the larger government forces offensive that was aimed at the liberation of Palmyra from ISIS occupation.

Into the second half of January 2016, opposition activity in the mountainous area in Jabal al-Akrad had decreased, this being attributed to the recent capture, by SDA units, of Salma settlement in Latakia Province. The 19 January MODRF briefing outlined continued cooperation between elements of what was being termed the 'Patriotic Opposition' and government forces backed by the Russian Aerospace Group in the fight against ISIS, Jabhat al-Nusra and other extremist groups. It was not all one way traffic however, opposition forces artillery and rocket fire being directed at a number of settlements under government control. The MODRF stated that "terrorist organizations Ashar ash-Sham and Jabhat al-Nusra conducted missile and artillery attacks on al-Faush and Kafr (Idlib Province)."

From January 22, there was a significant upsurge in the tempo of air operations, which were supporting intensified ground offensive operations by the SDA and allied groups in the area of Northern Latakia. On January 24 alone, some 24 towns and settlements were removed from opposition forces occupation, this including Rabia, which was considered an important point from which to launch further offensive operations.

It had, by this time, become clear that ISIS had not only lost the strategic initiative in Western Syria, but was in wholesale decline, certainly in regards to areas under its occupation. The main focus of ISIS offensive operations at this time were aimed at overrunning, or at least intensifying its siege of the government held areas of Deir ez-Zor in Eastern Syria.

Much of the Russian effort between 4-11 February was flown in support of the SDA, which, since the start of February, had recaptured some 800 square km of territory that encompassed 73 inhabited areas, allowing humanitarian aid to be delivered to these areas as well as basic amenities to be restored to the civil population.

The major ground operation conducted by SDA forces under the cover of Russian air strikes, was aimed at the liberation of Palmyra, which was accomplished in early March 2016, immediate plans being implemented shortly thereafter for the reduction in Russian air assets based in Syria.

5

CHRONOLOGY OF RUSSIAN AEROSPACE GROUP OPERATIONS IN SYRIA FROM 23 OCTOBER 2015 -15 MARCH 2016, WITH SPECIFICS OF SELECTED Su-24M OPERATIONS

For the most part the chronological order of dates will be the dates that the respective MODRF (Ministry Of Defence of the Russian Federation) briefing documents were issued, with an indication over the period that the briefing covered.

26 October 2015: The MODRF briefing for operations over the previous three days stated that Russian aircraft had flown 163 (later restated as 164) combat sorties, during the course of which 285 targets were engaged. Of these totals, 59 sorties had been conducted over the previous 24 hours, during the course of which 94 targets were engaged in the provinces of Hama, Idlib, Lattakia, Damascus, Aleppo and Deir ez-Zor. Much of the effort, it was emphasised, had targeted ISIS (Islamic State of Iraq and the Levant) and Jabhat al-Nusra groups.

An ISIS basing area, personnel and off-road vehicles configured with a plethora of weapons - large calibre machine guns, mortar tubes and ZU-23 23 mm caliber AA guns - was located by UAV (Uninhabited Air Vehicle) reconnaissance in a mountainous/wooded area near Khibrat al-Amai in Aleppo Province. Once the target validity had been verified a flight of two Su-24M's were tasked to attack it, resulting in the destruction of basing infrastructure and all of the vehicles present.

Su-24M operations over Eastern Syria resulted in an attack on an ISIS fortified position in the suburbs of Deir ez-Zor, the target being destroyed following the detonation of stored munitions.

28 October 2015: The MODRF briefing for operations over the previous 24 hours stated that Russian strike/attack aircraft had flown 71 combat sorties, during the course of which 118 targets were struck in the provinces of Idlib, Homs, Aleppo, Damascus and Lattakia. The main focus of attacks was centred on the interdiction of oil and munitions supply columns and infrastructure targets such as fortified positions and command centres. The increase in operational tempo, in regards to sortie numbers, was attributed to the uncovering of higher than normal numbers of targets by the various reconnaissance/surveillance assets at the Russians disposal.

A facility near Salma in Lattakia Province, described by the MORDF as a command and communications centre with an adjacent munitions depot, was detected by UAV reconnaissance. The validly of the target was further crosschecked and then allocated for attack by a flight of Su-24M's, resulting in its destruction. Su-24M's were also active over Aleppo Province, one such aircraft attacking a fortified position near Tel-Mregan. This particular fire position had enabled militants to exert control over the major roadway that was used to transport munitions and other supplies and to prevent the movement of refugees trying to flee the combat area. The Su-24M employed air bombs (type undisclosed) to destroy the positions fortifications and co-located vehicles armed with ZU-23 AA guns.

30 October 2016: The MODRF briefing by Chief of the Main Operational Directorate of the General Staff of the Russian Armed Forces, Andrei Kartapolov, for operations over the course of the month since the commencement of combat operations by the Russian Aerospace Group, stated that up to this date Russian aircraft had flown 1,391 combat sorties, during the course of which 1,623 targets had been engaged. The target list included, as laid down in Kartopolov's statement, "249 different command and communications centres; 51 terrorist training camps; 35 plants and workshops equipping cars with explosives; 131 ammunition depots; 371 strong points and fortified positions; 786 field camps and different bases".

2 November 2015: The MODRF briefing for operations over the previous two days stated that Russian aircraft had flown 131 combat sorties, during the course of which 237 targets were engaged in the provinces of Hama, Lattakia, Homs, Damascus, Aleppo and Raqqah. No specific details were released for operations by Su-24M aircraft.

3 November 2015: The MODRF briefing for operations, still ongoing at the time of the briefing, that day stated that Russian aircraft had flown 12 combat sorties engaging 24 targets that apparently included a command centre, a munitions depot, 10 fortified positions and 12 artillery and anti-aircraft artillery (probably employed in a surface to surface role) positions. No specific details were released for operations by Su-24M aircraft.

5 November 2015: The MODRF briefing for operations over the previous two days stated that Russian aircraft had flown 81 combat sorties, during the course of which 263 targets were engaged in the provinces of Hama, Lattakia, Homs, Damascus, Idlib, Aleppo, Raqqah and Deir ez-Zor.

Specific targets attacked by the Su-24M detachment included works for repairing armoured vehicles belonging to ISIS near Al-Nayrab airfield in Aleppo Province. Crosschecking of intelligence data had apparently confirmed that the workshops were used to repair armoured vehicles, including tanks, and for conversion of off-road vehicles to carry armament. A single Su-24M dropped a number of bombs (undetermined type), which destroyed the workshops, consisting of several buildings, and adjacent military hardware. An Su-24M attacked and destroyed a significant sized fortified area apparently occupied by ISIS forces. Post-strike OM (Objective Monitoring - damage assessment) confirmed that a tank, a ZU-23 twin AA artillery piece and a mortar battery were also destroyed.

Page 69-74: Su-24M operations out of Hmeymim air base in October-November 2015. MODRF

9 November 2015: The MODRF briefing for operations over the previous three days stated that Russian aircraft had flown 137 operational sorties, during the course of which 448 targets were engaged in the provinces of Aleppo, Damascus, Idlib, Latakia, Raqqah, Hama and Homs. The lower tempo of strike operations was explained, in part, by the fact that an increased number of aircraft of the Aerospace Group had been employed in a reconnaissance role, specifically acting upon data received from the information centre in Baghdad, Iraq, SDA (Syrian Democratic Army) ground forces facing ISIS and, apparently, some information which had been received by those opposition forces in conflict with ISIS. It would be pertinent then to assume that the reconnaissance sorties were not included in the above sortie numbers, which, it is inferred, relate only to strike sorties.

ISIS had, by this time, changed tactics as it adapted to the new threat that was introduced with the commencement of the Russian air campaign on 30 September. Whereas previously ISIS and other opposition groups, with a high degree of confidence, were able to absorb the low level of air strikes of the Syrian air force, and, particularly in areas where they were opposing Syrian Government forces, ISIS was faced with a negligible threat from the low tempo of air operations of the 'anti-ISIS coalition', they now had to adapt to a higher degree of maneuver operations and concealment to afford some protection against the Russian air strikes. The Russian air campaign had severely adversely impacted on the organisations fighting formations over the previous five weeks. Much of its resupply and reinforcement routes were only active at night in an attempt to afford a small measure of protection from the darkness.

During the period covered by the briefing an Su-24M bombed a target near Kafer Nbuda in Hama Province that was described by the MODRF as a workshop where armoured vehicles form the Jabhat al-Nusra group were repaired. Post-strike OM apparently showed that a hanger structure was destroyed, along with four tanks and a single IFV (Infantry Fighting Vehicle).

11 November 2015: The MODRF briefing for operations over the previous two days stated that Russian aircraft had flown 85 combat sorties, during the course of which 277 targets had been engaged in the provinces of Aleppo, Damascus, Latakia, Hama, Homs and Idlib. An increased tempo of reconnaissance sorties continued to be flown to aid in verification of data that was being received from some opposition groups, the Russian command no doubt being particularly skeptical of some of the information coming from groups involved in in-fighting with each other as well as against SDA forces.

A group of ISIS armoured vehicles, which had been located by UAV reconnaissance some 45 km to the south of Tadmor city in Homs Province, was attacked by at least one Su-24M. Post-strike OM showed that three tanks and two IFV's had been destroyed. Near Kafr Zita, in Hama Province, a Su-24M strike destroyed a Jabhat al-Nusra group mortar battery. Many of the strikes in Hama Province during the period covered in the briefing were aimed at thwarting a planned opposition offensive operation, information of which had been gathered through a number of channels.

13 November 2015: The MODRF briefing for operations over the previous two days, November 11 and 12, stated that Russian aircraft had flown 107 combat sorties, during the course of which 289 targets had been engaged in the provinces of Aleppo, Damascus, Idlib, Latakia, Hama, Homs, Daraa and Deir ez-Zor. The targets consisted of, as stated in the MODRF briefing document, "34 command and control centres... 16 POL [Petroleum Oil & Lubricants] and ammunition depots; 2 plants used for producing munitions and improvised explosives devices; 3 bases and terrorists training camps; 50 strong points with combat hardware and weapons and 184 fortified areas and defensive positions."

A strike was carried out by an Su-24M on what the MODRF described as an "ISIS strong point". Post-strike OM indicated that 3 mortar firing units, an ammunition storage facility and field fortifications had been destroyed.

18 November 2015: The MODRF briefing for operations conducted on the 17th stated that Russian aircraft had flown 127 combat sorties, including 29 long-range bomber sorties flown from Russian territory, the balance of 98 being flown by the Aerospace Group. There was an omission of data for the period of late on the 13th through 16 November, although it is known that the Russian Aerospace Group flew operations during this period.

19 November 2015: The briefing by Chief of the Main Operational Directorate of the General Staff of the Russian Armed Forces, Andrei Kartapolov, provided details of what was termed the second and third massive air strikes by long range aviation on targets in Syria, following the Long Range Aviation strikes conducted on the 17th. The strikes by Long Range Aviation carried out on the 18th, were flown from basing areas on Russian territory, supported by airstrikes launched by tactical combat aircraft based at Hmeymim. The briefing on the 19th stated that the previous day 126 sorties had been flown by Tu-160 and Tu-22M3 bombers, although the actual figure appears to have been 29 - 2 Tu-160, 3 Tu-95MS and 24 Tu-22M3, the balance being flown by the Aerospace Group (the actual value was 98 sorties flown by the Aerospace Group).

The third of the series of massive air strikes was conducted on 19 November. Details released indicate that Tu-95MS and Tu-160 strategic missile carrying aircraft launched 12 land attack cruise missiles against targets in Syria from 0900 until 09.20 MSK (Moscow time). The targets were indicated as ISIS facilities, including, as stated in the MODRF briefing, "POL depots; a plant producing explosives; a command centre, and an HQ of the ISIS terrorist organisation in the Idlib city". All targets struck were located in the provinces of Aleppo and Idlib.

Between 16.40 and 17.30 hours twelve Tu-22M3 bombers bombed 6 targets, stated by the MODRF to be ISIS controlled "... oil production sites... an ammunition depot and a workshop used for manufacturing and repairing mortars", all targets being located in the provinces of Raqqah and Deir ez-Zor.

The day's program called for 98 combat sorties to be flown by tactical aviation to strike 190 pre-selected targets. However, by the time of the briefing it was confirmed that only 60 sorties had been flown in which 138 targets had been struck.

Although daytime missions predominated, from early in the campaign the Aerospace Group began flying nighttime missions. Here Su-24M's White 75 and White 77 take-off from Hmeymim for a night mission configured with shoulder wing mounted external fuel tanks and OFAB-250-270 bombs. MODRF

20 November 2015: By 20 November the number of combat aircraft at the disposal of the Aerospace Group in Hmeymim was put at 69. Some 522 sorties had been flown since the 17th of the month, during the course of which 826 targets had been destroyed. It was also stated that 525 tanker trucks had been destroyed, it being unclear if one truck, in the view of the MORDF, constituted a single target or if that target constituted a grouping of trucks. It was estimated that 60,000 tons of oil had been destroyed, seriously degrading ISIS ability to generate finance to fund its campaigns in both Syria and Iraq.

Whilst specifics of air operations on the 20th were absent, the MODRF confirmed that 18 Kalibre land attack cruise missiles had been launched form warships of the Caspian Flotilla in the Caspian Sea against 7 targets located in the provinces of Raqqah, Idlib and Aleppo, around 1500 km or so distant.

23 November 2015: It was stated in an MODRF briefing report that over the course of the previous two days Russian aircraft had engaged 472 targets in the course 141 combat sorties in the provinces of Aleppo, Damascus, Idlib, Latakia, Hama, Homs, Raqqah and Deir ez-Zor. Oil related targets were struck in the districts of Raqqah, Palmyra and Deir ez-Zor. The oil interdiction campaign had, according to the MODRF statements, destroyed in excess of 1,000 petrol/oil transport vehicles, as well as a number of fixed oil installations. The most significant losses to the opposition groups, in particular ISIS, occurred in the provinces of Deir ez-Zor, Raqqah and Aleppo, the vicinity of this latter city being the location of a strike on opposition forces command and control infrastructure. Other areas struck included Serakab in Idlib Province and Qalaat al-Madiq in Hama Province, opposition forces apparently abandoning their positions in these areas following the air attacks.

23-26 November 2015: During this period Russian aircraft engaged 449 targets in the course of 134 sorties in the provinces of Aleppo, Damascus, Idlib, Latakia, Hama, Homs, Raqqah and Deir-ez-Zor. An Su-24M hit an ISIS underground munitions storage facility located in the suburbs of Al-Qaryatayn in Homs Province. The target was hit by a single OFAB-250-270 bomb, the resultant detonation triggering a chain of explosions as munitions were set off. On the 24th, a Su-24M, one of a flight of two such aircraft, was shot down over Northern Syria by a Turkish Air Force F-16. Details of this operation and its aftermath are covered in chapter 6.

4 December 2015: The MODRF briefing for operations conducted between 26 November and 4 December stated that Russian aircraft had flown 431 combat sorties, during the course of which 289 targets were engaged in the provinces of Aleppo, Idlib, Latakia, Hama, Homs, Raqqah and Deir ez-Zor. It was disclosed at the briefing that during the course of the previous week Russian aircraft had destroyed 8 oil fields and 12 oil and gas transfer stations and in excess of 170 tanker trucks as the oil interdiction campaign continued.

White 72 lands at Hmeymim following a bombing mission. MODRF

Su-24M White 75 with a load of 4 x OFAB-250-270 HE bombs. MODRF

8 December 2015: The MODRF briefing for operations conducted over the previous four days stated that Russian aircraft had flown 300 combat sorties (includes sorties by Tu-22M3 intermediate range bombers based on Russian territory). In addition four cruise missiles were launched form the Russian Federation Navy Submarine *Rostov on Don* submerged in the Mediterranean Sea off the coast of Syria. No specific information was released about Su-24M operations.

9 December 2015: The MODRF briefing for operations conducted over the previous 24 hours stated that Russian aircraft had flown 82 combat sorties, during the course of which 204 targets had been engaged in the provinces of Aleppo, Idlib, Latakia, Hama and Homs. Thirty two of the 82 sorties had been flown during the hours of darkness. No specific information was released about Su-24M operations.

15 December 2015: A briefing by the Chief of the Main Operational Directorate of the Russian General Staff, Sergie Rudskov, provided a summary of the Russian Aerospace Groups operations since they had commenced on 30 September that year. The main point was the sortie total of 4,201 (this included 145 sorties flown by Russian Long Range Aviation assets based in Russian territory). The briefing also outlined that operations flown over the past three days had targeted, among other things, the ISIS controlled oil infrastructure and distribution networks. Specifically this was detailed as six facilities producing oil and seven separate convoys of oil tankers that were transporting crude oil to distribution centres outside Syrian territory. It was noted that since the commencement of the oil interdiction campaign Russian aircraft had, by that time, destroyed in excess of 1,200 tanker trucks.

Page 82-86: Series of stills from an onboard camera system showing various segments of a typical Su-24M mission over Syria in 2015/16. MODRF

16 December 2015: The MODRF briefing for operations conducted over the previous 24 hours stated that Russian aircraft had flown 59 combat sorties, during the course of which 212 targets had been engaged in the provinces of Aleppo, Idlib, Latakia, Hama, Homs, Hasakah and Raqqah. Information furnished by the MODRF indicated that opposition fielded forces suffered several hundred personnel casualties and the destruction of two tanks, one infantry fighting vehicle, fifteen off-road vehicles, armed with large caliber machine guns, and around 16 other vehicles.

ISIS fielded forces were attacked by a Su-24M in Aleppo Province resulting in a number of casualties and the destruction of three vehicles armed with large caliber machine guns. Another Su-24M attack was directed against a target described by the MODRF as an ISIS "hidden base" near to the settlement of Al-Karatein in Homs Province. The hidden base, stated by MODRF to contain "a command centre, an ammunition depot and barracks" in underground shelters, was apparently destroyed by a number of BETAB-500 concrete penetrating air bombs dropped by one or more Su-24M's.

25 December 2015: The MODRF briefing, by the Chief of the Main Operational Directorate of the Russian General Staff, provided a summary of the Russian Aerospace Groups operations since they had commenced on 30 September that year. The main point was the sortie total of 5,240 (this total included the 145 sorties flown by Russian Long Range Aviation assets based in Russian territory).

It was noted that during the previous week leading up to the 25th, the oil interdiction campaign, with input from the Su-24M detachment, had resulted in the destruction of 37 ISIS oil production/refining facilities and 17 convoys transporting oil across Syria's borders. It was further noted that around 2,000 oil transport trucks had been destroyed, up to that date.

One of the major oil transportation routes, detailed by the MODRF, led "from the [ISIS controlled areas] Deir ez-Zor Province, through Guna and Tel Sfuk [Syria] in direction to Mosul and Zakho on the territory of Iraq." The main border crossing point for the illegal oil transports, it was stated, was "near Tel Sfuk". The Russian report reiterated that Turkey remained the key destination for the illegal oil trafficking, which crossed into Turkey from Iraq at the Zakho checkpoint, it being stated in the briefing document that this route "coincides with the so-called 'Eastern' route". Satellite photographic images presented by the MODRF purported to show vast numbers of oil tanker trucks on both sides of the Iraq-Turkey border near Zakho. The MODRF stated that by the time the presented images were taken "there had been 11,775 oil trucks and heavy vehicles on both sides of the Turkish-Iraq borderline, 4,350 of them were in Turkey, 7,245... in Iraq". Further photographic analysis showed what was purported by the MODRF to be 3,850 oil transport trucks and other heavy vehicles on the Turkish side of the border. Some 200 of these were moving in the direction of the Iraq border with Turkey. A further image, labelled 'area B', purported to show an area close to the Iraq-Turkey border with 980 trucks on the Iraq side and 680 trucks on the Turkish side. Further images showed additional trucks, numbering in excess of 6,000, apparently in holding areas as they waited their turn to cross the border.

Su-24M White 71 at Hmeymim air base in late 2015/early 2016. This aircraft is armed with BETAB-500 concrete penetrating bombs. MODRF

Su-24M's White 79 (top) and White 72 (bottom) at Hmeymim in late 2015/early 2016.
MODRF

In addition to the Eastern routes ISIS also transported oil through Northern and Western routes, mostly during the hours of darkness, although this was no real cover from observation from modern surveillance systems. In a further effort to conceal the movements from Russian observation, oil trucks were, on occasion, disguised to look like standard heavy transport vehicles and convoys were being broken up into smaller groups to limit losses in the event of discovery and attack. There had, over recent weeks, been a significant reduction in the volume of tanker trucks using the Northern route that followed a direction leading to the oil refinery at Batman. There was also a decrease in oil traffic on the Western route that followed the direction of Reyhanli – Iskanderun. However, there was a noted increase in the numbers of oil trucks in the vicinity of the port of Dortyol in Turkey, the MODRF pointing the finger of complicity in the illegal oil trade at Turkey, a major factor in the vastly increased tensions between those two nations over the previous few months.

The briefing went on to state that "on the previous day [24 December], 189 strikes were made….", of which 142 were pre-planned strikes while the remaining 47 were against targets detected during what was termed 'duty mission'. This latter mission type was most often used against opposition fielded forces in support of ground operations by the SDA.

29 December 2015: The MORF briefing for operations conducted over the three days since 25 February stated that Russian aircraft, in an increased tempo of strike operations, had flown 164 combat sorties, during the course of which 556 targets were engaged in the provinces of Aleppo, Idlib, Latakia, Hama, Homs, Damascus, Raqqah and Deir ez-Zor. No specific details of Su-24M operations were released for this period.

30 December 2015: The MODRF briefing for operations over the two days since the 28th, stated that Russian aircraft had flown 164 combat sorties, during the course of which 424 targets were engaged in the provinces of Aleppo, Idlib, Latakia Hama, Homs, Damascus, Daraa, Raqqah and Deir ez-Zor. During this period, information furnished by opposition forces, after further verification as to its validity, resulted in a Su-24M strike that destroyed a munitions depot belonging to the Jabhat al-Nusra group near to al-Zerba.

The oil interdiction campaign continued with six incidences of air attacks on oil transportation vehicles in Deir ez-Zor and Aleppo Provinces. Although the type of aircraft was undisclosed, this was most likely Su-24M or Su-34.

11 January 2016:, The MODRF briefing for operations conducted over the first ten days of 2016 stated that Russian aircraft had flown 311 combat sorties, during the course of which 1,097 targets were engaged in the provinces of Aleppo, Idlib, Latakia, Hama, Homs, Damascus, Hasakah, Daraa, Raqqah and Deir ez-Zor. Among the main target sets were opposition forces infrastructure and deployed groupings, as well as a continuation of the oil interdiction campaign, which concentrated on attacks on oil production facilities. No specific details of Su-24M operations were released for this period.

Su-24M's White 80 (top) and White 49 (above) at Hmeymim in late 2015/early 2016. These aircraft are armed with a typical load of 4 x OFAB-250-270 bombs. MODRF

Top: Su-25M White 75 at Hmeymim air base with the S-400 'Triumph' long-range air defence missiles forming a backdrop. Above: Su-24M White 76 lands back at Hmeymim air base following a strike mission. MODRF

19 January 2016: The MODRF briefing for operations over the previous four days stated that Russian aircraft had flown 157 combat sorties, during the course of which 579 targets were engaged in the provinces of Aleppo, Raqqah, Latakia, Homs, Hama and Deir ez-Zor. The oil interdiction campaign continued to reduce the source of revenue available to ISIS and other prescribed terrorist organisations. Among the targets bombed were what the MODRF described as "a large POL storage and oil pumping station" located in Raqqah Province. This facility was bombed sometime between the 15th and 19th of January. A large column of oil trucks transporting oil towards the Turkish border was detected near Harbul, Aleppo Province. A Su-24M was directed to attack the column, resulting in the destruction of 23 oil tanker trucks.

20 January 2016: The MODRF briefing for operations over the course of the last day stated that Russian aircraft had flown 16 combat sorties, during the course of which 57 targets were engaged. The reduction in daily sortie levels was principally attributed to adverse weather over much of Syria, which led to operations being flown only over the provinces of Latakia and Deir ez-Zor. No specific details of Su-24M operations were released for this period.

25 January 2016: The MODRF briefing for operations over the course of 22-24 January stated that Russian aircraft had flown 169 combat sorties, during the course of which 484 targets were engaged. No specific details of Su-24M operations were released for this period.

2 February 2016: The MODRF briefing for operations over the previous week stated that Russian aircraft had flown 468 combat sorties, during the course of which 1,354 targets had been struck in the provinces of Aleppo, Latakia, Hama, Homs, Damascus, Raqqah, Daraa and Deir ez-Zor. The above sortie total included 24 sorties by Tu-22M3 intermediate range bombers flown direct from Russian territory.

The major operation during this period was to relive pressure on the eastern bastion of Deir ez-Zor, which had been besieged by ISIS forces and was under heavy direct assault as ISIS attempted to capture the town. The air operations over Deir included air drops of humanitarian supplies to the inhabitants of the town by Syrian Air Force transport aircraft employing Russian supplied P-7 parachute-platforms. During the period Su-24M strike aircraft were also heavily involved in operations against opposition forces that had retreated into mountainous areas of Latakia Province.

One mission outlined in the Russian briefing concerned an attack by a Su-24M strike on what was described as a "field camp" near the settlement of Kinsibba that was occupied by a group of militants originating from CIS (Commonwealth of Independent States – former Soviet Republics) territory. This group, which had apparently crossed the border from Turkey into Syria, had been monitored by UAV reconnaissance (the Russian UAV operated over Syria supplemented space based and other reconnaissance means such as ELNT – Electronic Intelligence). Furnished with the necessary targeting data Su-24M strike aircraft dropped ordnance inflicting a stated 17 casualties.

Page 94 top: A Su-24M armed with OFAB-250-270 bombs commences its take-off run at Hmeymim air base. Page 94 bottom and page 95: Su-24M and Su-25's at dispersal at Hmeymim. Above: Su-24M White 49 taxis at Hmeymim. MODRF

A POL storage facility near Jeb Ghabishah in Aleppo Province, which the MODRF stated was under ISIS control, was destroyed by munitions launched form a Su-24M. A target set described by the MODRF as a fuel station and a POL storage facility near to Jabal Batra, Damascus Province, was attacked by a Su-24M. This facility, which the MODRF stated belonged to the Jaysh al-Islam group, was deemed to have been completely destroyed by post-strike OM, which confirmed a direct hit by at least one bomb.

4 February 2016: The MODRF briefing for operations over the three day period covering 1-4 February 2016, stated that Russian aircraft had flown 237 combat sorties, during the course of which 875 targets had been engaged in the provinces of Aleppo, Latakia, Homs, Hama and Deir ez-Zor. Over the previous day or so, ground operations by the SDA, aided by loyal paramilitary groups, broke through to the settlements of Nubul and Al-Zahra, which had been besieged by opposition forces for 4 years.

11 February 2016: The MODRF briefing for operations over the previous week, 4-11 February, stated that Russian aircraft had, over that period, flown 510 combat sorties, during the course of which 1,888 targets had been struck in the provinces of Aleppo, Hama, Latakia, Daraa, Hasakah, Raqqah and Deir ez-Zor. An attack by a Su-24M resulted in the destruction of what was stated by the MODRF to be an ISIS command centre in Idlib Province.

Page 97-99: Series of photographs of Su-24M's at Hmeymim armed with BETAB-500 concrete penetrating bombs employed for the destruction of underground facilities and fortifications. MODRF

Russian Aerospace Group Su-24M White 76 lands at Hmeymim air base in early 2016. MODRF

16 February 2016: The MODRF briefing for operations over the period of 10-16 February stated that Russian aircraft had flown 444 combat sorties, during the course of which 1,593 targets had been engaged in the provinces of Aleppo, Daraa, Hama, Homs, Latakia and Deir ez-Zor. The upsurge in operations had come after a framework agreement to wind down Russian combat operations in Syria was effectively put on hold as many of the opposition groups mistakenly saw this as an opportunity to increase militaristic activity in the North and South of Syria. Much of this increased activity was associated with infighting between various groupings in the provinces of Aleppo and Idlib, each vying to control whatever piece of territory they either held or could capture prior to any ceasefire agreement taking effect.

Tensions in the North were further exacerbated by Turkish army artillery strikes, apparently commencing around 14 February, which the MODRF stated were concentrated against Syrian Democratic Army and allied forces in border areas, as well as against inhabited settlements. In the latter regard the MODRF claimed to have monitored no less than 100 Turkish army artillery rounds impacting on inhabited areas of Aleppo Province.

In concert with its military campaign in the North of Syria, the Turkish government ratcheted up the anti-Russian war of words with further accusations against Russia; Turkey ever fearful that it could lose its grip over those areas of Northern Syria that it either controlled directly or by the use of proxy organisations inside Syria's borders. This disinformation campaign ranged from the usual unfounded rhetoric about Russian air operations striking only civilian targets to, as noted by the MODRF, the launching of a ballistic missile against a hospital in Idlib

Province by a warship of the Russian Caspian Flotilla – no such attack having taken place, indeed, no such capability existing for Caspian Flotilla warships.

24 February: In line with the desire to implement a ceasefire that it was hoped could lead to a peace settlement, Russia significantly relaxed the tempo of air operations over Syria during the period 22-24 February 2016, with only 62 combat sorties being flown, during the course of which 187 targets were engaged in the provinces of Aleppo, Hama, Homs, Raqqah and Deir ez-Zor as operations were still flown against groups excluded from the ceasefire, ISIS, Jabhat al-Nusra and certain other extremist groups, which were to be excluded from any proposed peace deal.

During the period covered in the briefing document few details were forthcoming about specific Su-24M operations. An ISIS concentration of personnel and hardware, located near al-Bab in Aleppo Province, was attacked by a Su-24M. Post-strike OM indicated that, as well as personnel casualties, no less than three vehicles, armed with large caliber machine guns, were destroyed.

3 March 2016: The Russian Defence Minister, General of the Army, Sergei Shoigu, announced that, in accordance with an order issued by the Supreme Commander-in-Chief of the Armed Forces, Vladimir Putin, a significant element of the Russian Armed Forces Grouping would be redeployed back to bases in the Russian interior commencing on the 15th of the Month.

The first such group of aircraft, Su-34's, to leave Syria did so on 15 March, under navigational escort of a Tupolev Tu-154 transport aircraft leader. Each of the combat aircraft would follow the Tu-154 formation leader until within the borders of the Russian Federation where after they would proceed independently to their respective bases. If deemed necessary, the aircraft could conduct intermediate stops for refueling or for any technical issues that may have arisen over the 5000+ km flights.

The second group of combat aircraft to leave Syria consisted of several Su-25SM's under the navigational escort of an Ilyushin Il-76 transport aircraft leader, departing Syria on 16 March. The third group, this time consisting of several Su-24M's, departed Syria later on the 16th, under the navigational escort of a Il-76 transport aircraft leader.

In May 2016, less than two months after the Russian withdrawal of a large segment of its aviation assets from Syria, the Supreme Commander-in-Chief of the Russian Armed Forces, in summing up the operation to that time, noted that some 10,000 combat sorties had been flown, during which 30,000 targets had been engaged, including 200 oil infrastructure targets.

As this volume was prepared in early 2017, the musings of a new peace deal between the Syrian government and western backed opposition groups held hope of a permanent peace in Syria between western backed opposition groups and the Syrian government. Only time will tell if the tenuis ceasefires will lead to such a peace that would allow the Syrian government forces, backed by the Russian Federation to turn its full attention to eradicating ISIS in the Syrian Arab Republic.

Page 102-110: Series of photographs of the first batch of Su-24M's to return to Russia, still at Hmeymim and having returned to Russia on 16 March 2016. The bottom photograph on page 106 shows the Il-76 transport aircraft, RF-76770, which accompanied the Su-24Ms as a navigational escort. MODRF

6

THE SHOOTDOWN OF WHITE 83

On 24 November 2015, a Russian Aerospace Group Su-24M strike aircraft, operating out of Hmeymim air base in the Syrian Arab Republic, was shot down by a Turkish Air Force (Türk Hava Kuvvetleri) Lockheed Martin F-16 'Fighting Falcon' fighter/interceptor aircraft during a bombing attack just inside the Syrian-Turkish border. This incident immediately caused a major international incident with Russia demanding an explanation as to why the incident occurred and Turkey claiming the Su-24M was over Turkish airspace at the time.

In the hours following the incident the Defence Attaché from the Embassy of the Republic of Turkey was most urgently summoned to the Russian Ministry of Defence. On arrival he was formally presented with an official protest concerning the actions of Turkey. This protest contained the following statement reproduced here verbatim:

"Today at 10.30 the Russian aircraft, which performed combat counterterrorist missions was shot down by an aircraft of the Turkish Air Force.

The Russian aircraft did not cross the Turkish border and acted only against objects on the territory of Syria. Combat actions of the Russian aviation were conducted against illegal terrorist formations, which consist of a large number of militants from the Russian North Caucasus.

Efforts of the Russian Defence Ministry specialists to organise cooperation with the Turkish party by emergency communications link were not successful.

The Defence Ministry considers actions of the Turkish Air Force as an unfriendly act.

At present the Russian Defence Ministry is designing a complex of measures directed to respond such incidents.

Combat missions against terrorists in Syria will be continued".

Later on the 24th, details of what had transpired were provided by the Russian Chief of the Main Operational Directorate of the General Staff of the Russian Armed Forces, Lt. General Sergei Rudskoy, who stated:

"Today, at 10.24 (MKS [Moscow time]) an F-16 fighter of the Turkish Air Force shot down Su-24M tactical bomber of the Russian Aerospace Forces, which was performing a combat sortie over the territory of the Syrian Arab Republic. The fighter supposedly performed the strike with IR [Infrared] homing headed short-range missile [This was apparently an AIM-9L].

The objective monitoring data confirmed that the Turkish warplane did not make any attempt to establish a communications or visual contact with the Russian bomber.

The missile hit the Su-24M aircraft over the territory of Syria. The bomber crash place is on the territory of Syria four kilometers far from the borderline. The Su-24M crew managed to eject. According to the preliminary data, fire from the ground killed one of the pilots.

The objective monitoring data shows that the Russian aircraft did not cross the Turkish borderline. Data received by [from] the Syrian Air Defence Forces confirmed this fact as well.

Moreover, radar reconnaissance data, which was received from the Hmeymim airbase, registered Syrian airspace violation by the attacking aircraft of the Turkish Air Force.

This fact is assessed as a flagrant violation of international law with extremely grave consequences and the direct breach of Memorandum on air incident prevention and flight safety over the Syrian Arab Republic, which had been signed by the USA and relevant for all countries of the coalition, including Turkey.

That is why the Turkish party started urgent consultations with the NATO instead of immediate contacting with the Russian Defence Ministry.

Defence Attaché of Turkey in the Russian Federation was presented a decisive protest against the actions of the Turkish Air Force, which had led to the loss of the Russian aircraft.

It is to be mentioned that from the beginning of the operation, the Russian Defence Ministry had established a direct telephone line between the National Centre for State Defence Control of the Russian Federation and the Ministry of National Defence of Turkey. But it has no practical use due to the fault of the Turkish party.

In order to evacuate the Russian pilots from the landing point, a search and rescue operation was conducted by two Mi-8 helicopters. In the course of the operation, one of the helicopters was damaged by small arms fire and performed an emergency landing in the neutral area. One… member of Marine Troops – was killed.

The personnel of the search and rescue team and the helicopter crew were evacuated and are now at the Hmeymim airbase. The helicopter was destroyed by mortar fire conducted from the territory controlled by illegal armed groups."

On 25 November the Russian Military attaché went to the General Staff of the Turkish Armed Forces on the understanding that he would receive access to alleged conversations between the Turkish F-16 crews and the crews of the Russian Su-24M prior to the shoot down. However, on arrival he was informed that the material, which Russia asserted did not exist, would not be made available.

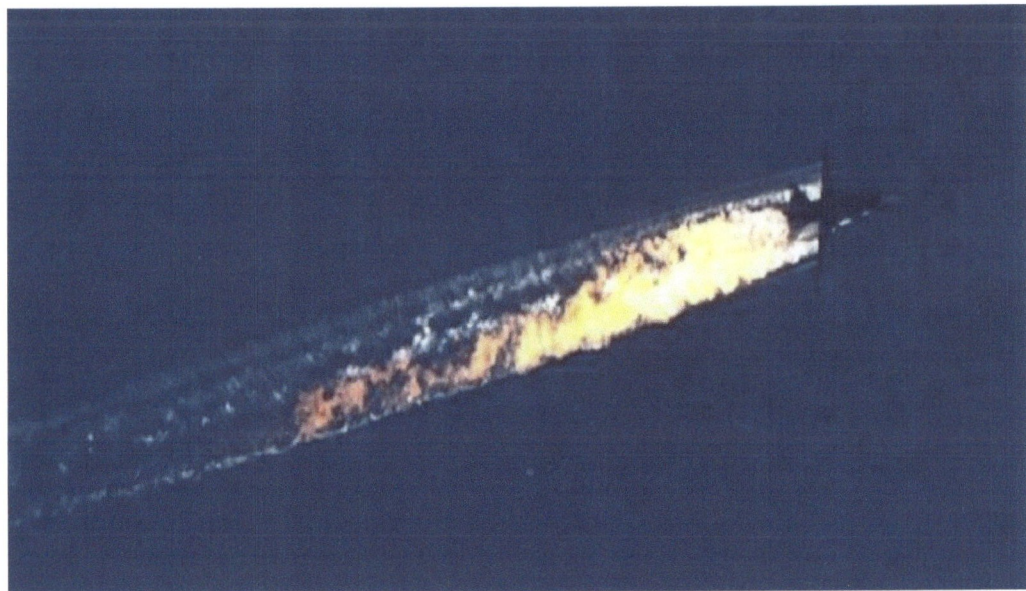

Top: Su-24M White 83 trailing a PTK-6M type braking parachute after landing at Hmeymim air base following a mission prior to the fateful mission of 24 November 2015. MODRF Above: Video still from news broadcast of footage, purportedly emanating from Syrian opposition forces, showing White 83 as the aircraft plummets to the ground on fire after being struck by an AIM-9L infrared guided air to air missile launched by a Turkish Air Force F-16C fighter aircraft.

It was naturally inevitable that different versions of why the incident occurred and what actually transpired would emerge in the days following. The Turkish side stated that a patrol of F-16C interceptors was vectored to the area of the Syrian-Turkish border to identify and turn back a Russian strike aircraft that had crossed the border into Turkey. The Russian side stating that it was a pre-planned ambush against the Su-24M strike aircraft, tail number 83, that NATO had been informed by Russia was operating on the Syrian side of the border. Certainly within NATO countries it was being touted as an act of Russian aggression countered by an extreme vigilance of North Atlantic Treaty Organisation external borders, in this case that of Turkey. However, despite the lukewarm statements of solidarity between the remaining NATO partners and Turkey, the holes in the story were far too large for any credibility to stick, even in those first days following the incident.

On 27 November, the Commander-in-Chief of the Russian Aerospace Forces held a briefing to put forward the facts from the Russian side on the shooting down of the Russian Su-24M, this 'statement of facts' about the incident being here reproduced verbatim:

"At 9.15 [09.15] (MSK) it [Su-24M White 83] was assigned to strike near Kepir-Motlu-Zahiya, located in the north of Syria.

This task was assigned to two Su-24M aircraft crews, including one of pilot Lieutenant Colonel Oleg Peshkov and Captain Konstantin Murakhtin (aircraft number 83, with combat payload of four OFAB-250-270 air bombs).

The crews were assigned to conduct combat air patrol near Maarat al-Numan at flight levels of 5800 m and 5650 m…

The aircraft took off from Hmeymim airbase at 9.42 [09.42].

At 9.52 [09.52], the Su-24M entered detection zone of Turkish Air Force radar means and was under their coverage in the course of 34 minutes.

After 20 minutes passed since the crew had entered its area of responsibility, the Command centre of the Hmeymim airbase ordered it to eliminate militants in the area.

The crews bombed two assigned targets and turned to the left to make another approach for destruction of two remaining targets.

As it was carrying out an airstrike at the target located 5.5 km to the south of the Turkish border, at 10.24 the crew led by Lieutenant Colonel Peshkov O.A. launched bombs at the target and was then downed by an 'air-to-air' missile from an F-16 fighter of the Turkish Air Force, which had performed take-off from Diyarbakir airfield of the 8th airbase located in the territory Turkey.

During the analysis of video air situation display provided by the Command Centre of the Syrian Air Force and Air Defence, an aerial target was spotted, moving from Turkey in the direction of the state border at the speed of 810 kmph [km/h] and with the heading of 190 degrees.

After the Turkish fighter approached the Su-24M at a range equal to the range of a missile launch (equal to 5-7 km), which proves that the F-16 was in the Syrian air space), it quickly maneuvered to the right, lowered, and disappeared from the display of the air situation display.

According to the objective monitoring data received from the air defence means, while the Russian bomber did not cross the Turkish border.

The crew of the leading aircraft confirms the missile launch. After the launch and a left turn for heading 130 degrees, they observed a flash and a trail of white smoke, which he reported to the flight control officer.

At 10.25, the flight control officer registered that the mark from the Su-24M aircraft disappeared from the radars. The further requests and the requests of the leader crew of the Lieutenant Colonel Peshkov remained without answer.

The estimated time of arrival of an F-16 aircraft from the military airfield Diyarbakir from the stand-by position on the ground to the possible place of missile launch constitutes 46 minutes (15 minutes for preparation and take-off, 31 minutes – the flight time needed to arrive at the firing point).

Thus, interception of the Su-24M aircraft from the stand-by position on the ground form the military airfield Diyarbakir is impossible as the necessary time for approaching the target exceeds the minimum time needed for attack by 12 minutes.

Objective monitoring data received from the Syrian radar stations confirmed the presence of two F-16's in the duty zone form 9.11 [09.11] till 10.26 min (for 1 h 15 min) at the altitude of 2400 metres that shows that the operation was planned beforehand and the fighters were ready to attack from the air ambush over the territory of Turkey.

It is to be mentioned that the fighter aircraft stopped maneuvering in the duty zone an[d] headed rapidly to the offset point 1 minute and 40 seconds before the maximum approach of the Su-24M aircraft to the Syrian-Turkish border. The method the F-16 aircraft entered the engagement zone (not by the curve of pursuit) shows that it was vectored from the ground.

Actions of the Turkish aircraft after launching of the missiles over the territory of Syria – the wind-down turn with loss of altitude and going under the lower range line of the air defence means – also speaks for the fact that the perfidious crew's actions were planned beforehand.

Objective monitoring data form the Hmeymim airbase and the leader aircraft did not register any request made by the crew of the Turkish aircraft to the Russian pilots on the pre-arranged frequency.

The readiness of the Turkish media to cover this incident is also surprising…

… Since the signing of the mutual understanding memorandum between the Russian Ministry of Defence and the Department of Defence of the USA on October 23, 2015, the Command of the Russian air group has undeviatingly taken all measures to prevent incidents between Russian military aircraft and warplanes belonging to the coalition countries.

In accordance with these agreements, the Russian Air Force Command Centre at Hmeymim airbase had informed representatives of the US Air Force concerning the engagement areas and echelons of a pair of Su-24M bombers in advance."

Turkish officials made various statements indicating that they had not actually identified the aircraft were dismissed by Russia as Turkey, along with other coalition members, had prior been provided details of the Su-24M patrol area by the Russian Command.

Flight chart of Turkish F-16 fighter after taking off from Diyarbakır air base

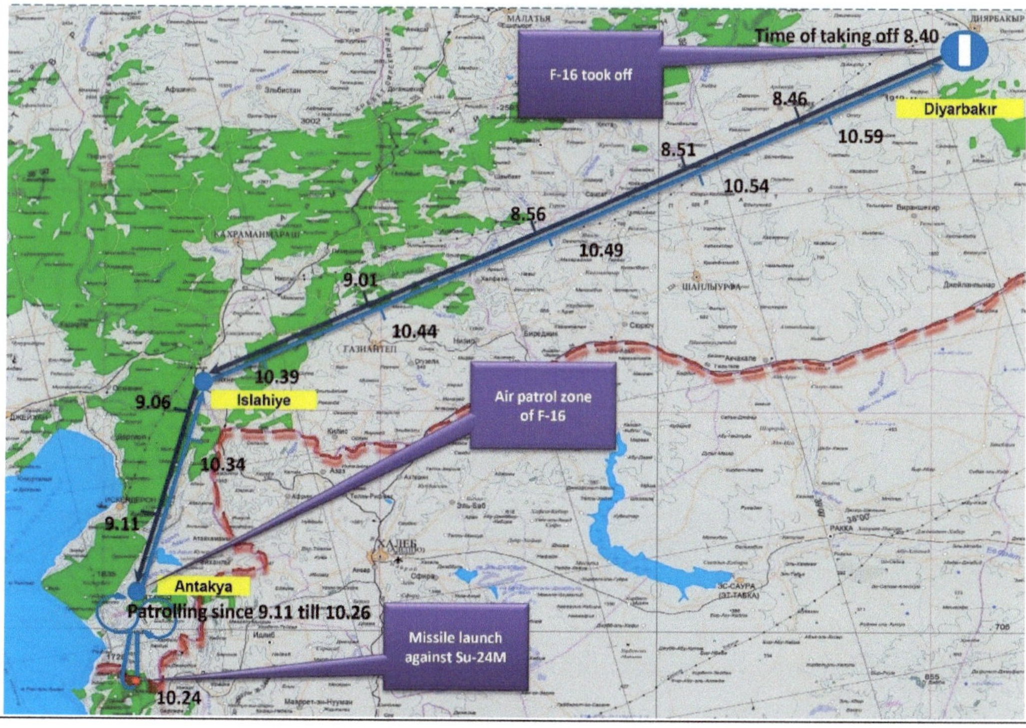

Elimination chart of the Russian Su-24M

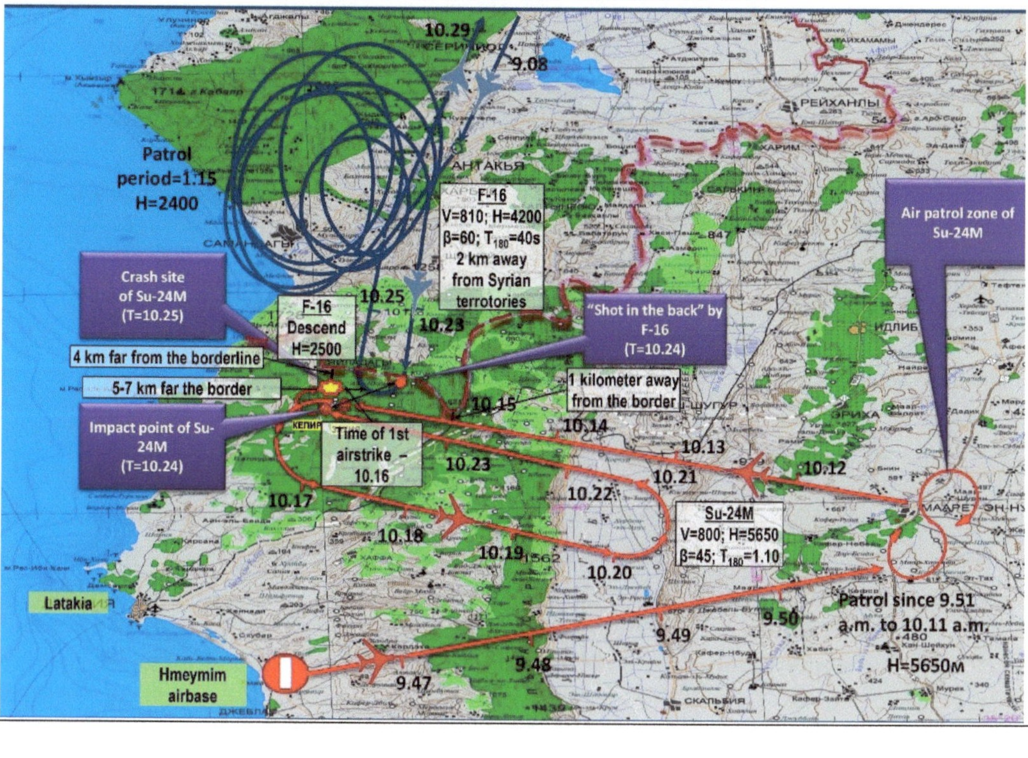

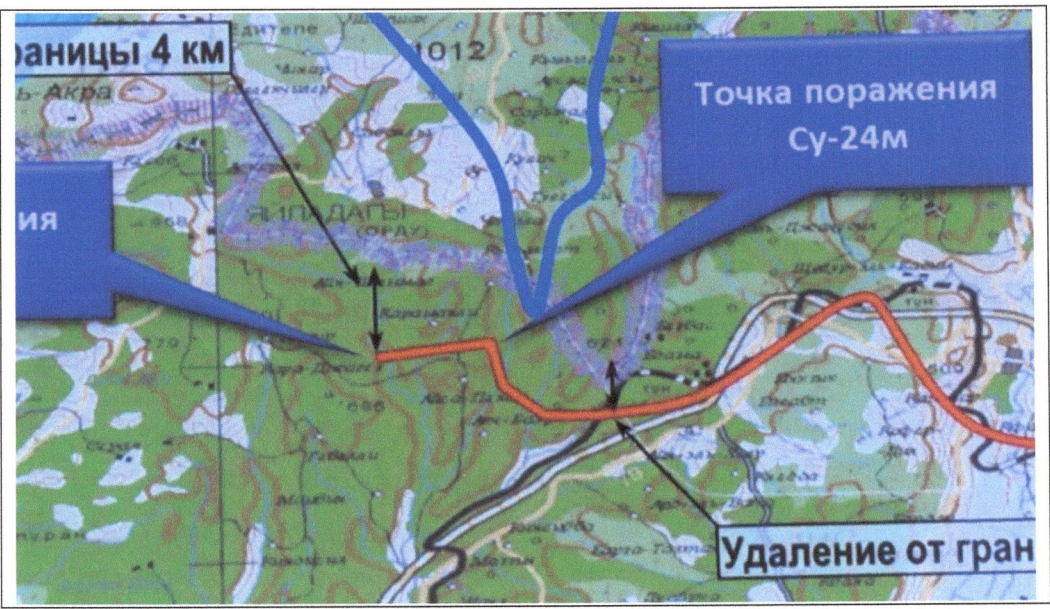

Previous page top: Flight chart of the various timings and positions of the Turkish F-16C after taking off from Diyarbakir air base in Turkey. Previous page bottom: Flight chart showing the timings and positions of the various aircraft involved in the incident that led to the shoot down of the Russian Su-24M. Above: Flight chart showing the positions of the Su-24M relevant to the Turkey-Syria border at the time it was shot down by the missile launched from the Turkish F-16. MODRF

The crew of the stricken Su-24M had successfully ejected, but the pilot was killed by small arms fire as he descended, the navigator reaching terra firma safely.

A military operation to rescue the surviving crew member from the Su-24M lasted for some 12 hours through the night of 24-25 November 2015. The initial attempt to extract the navigator, Murakhtin, had failed under the intense fire of opposition forces, a helicopter being lost in the process as noted above. Russian casualties included one fatality. A larger scale joint Russian/SDA (Syrian Democratic Army) recuse operation was launched, leading to the successful extraction of the navigator under cover of darkness. As the rescue areas was a hive of activity with significant numbers of opposition forces having been drawn in for the purpose of killing the crewman, air strikes and artillery fire was called down on those groups trying to find the Russian navigator, resulting in undetermined casualties.

Any short term symbolic victory the opposition forces hay have felt they had won with the killing of the Russian pilot as he descended, was short lived, The end result of the rescue operations that followed was a hastening of the SDA offensive operations to take control of the area, opposition forces being pushed out as the rescue operation itself had become a precursor for a larger Syrian government forces/Russian operation to gain control over the mountainous area of northern Latakia Province, effectively removing one of the cross border areas in which opposition groups received arms and reinforcements across the Turkish/Syrian border.

There was a distinct lack of 'anti-ISIS coalition' offer of assistance in the search and recovery of the remaining crewman who was being hunted by the militants on the ground, nor was there any apparent coalition attempt to restrain the militants they were supporting financially and materially. What was not in short supply, however, was a swath of support for Turkey, on the surface at least, from other NATO nations and coalition partners with statements to the effect that Turkey had the right to defend her borders. However, it was clear, even in the first hours following the incident, that all was not as it seemed with the Turkish statement that it had fired a missile at an unidentified aircraft that it determined had crossed its border for a mere 17 seconds.

It is certainly clear that the norms of international law regarding the interception of an unidentified aircraft that has either crossed or is approaching to imminently cross a national border, were completely disregarded. This fact alone made what side of the border the incident had taken place on a moot point. There was, as noted above, no western government condemnation of the shooting of the pilot as he descended after ejecting from the stricken aircraft. Nor was there, in the weeks that followed, any willingness to hand over the person responsible for killing the pilot, whom had fled across the border to Turkey. This prevailed even after that person was under the guard of the Turkish authorities for crimes committed in Turkey.

Few serious voices within NATO could have been under the illusion that a hit and run incident to shoot down a Russian aircraft over Syria, under the pretense of self-defence, would have had real detrimental effect on the Russian operations in Syria. However, there were self-misleading voices that felt that such an incident was a symbolic victory over a resurgent Russia. Nothing, however, could have been further from the truth. In the immediate aftermath, Russia, voicing its heartfelt opinion that it could not reply on western powers adherence to the Memorandum of understanding regarding the avoidance of air incidents and flight safety over Syria, announced that it would take unilateral measures to ensure the safety of its aircraft. The most immediate of those actions was the provision of Su-30SM advanced fighter aircraft protection for Russian strike aircraft operating near the borders with Turkey. The next measure was to move the Russian Navy Missile Cruiser *Moskva*, armed with the 'Fort' air defence system – analogues to the S-300 long-range SAM (Surface to Air Missile), to take up a station on combat alert off the Syrian Latakia coast, specifically to provide air defence for Hmeymim air base.

These deployments came with a 25 November warning, issued by the MODRF, that from that point onwards "all potentially dangerous targets will be destroyed". All contacts with Turkey were severed at a military level, reinforcing the threat that Turkish aircraft positioning themselves to threaten Russian air operations would be engaged without any consultation.

The end result of the incident, in regards to the strategic situation in the air over Syria, was its facilitation upon Russia being able to assert its control over most of Syria's airspace, for on 26 November an S-400 (widely regarded to be the most capable surface to air missile system in operational service) long-range surface to air missile detachment was put on combat alert at Hmeymim with Pantsir-S1 short-range Missile/Gun air defence systems for close base protection. This caused immediate concern within NATO, which was forced to more or less cede full control of the airspace of Eastern Syria to Russia as it had no counter to such modern air defence systems. Russian anger was further stoked when the United States Embassy in Moscow issued a statement containing the following quote forwarded by the MODRF "the deployment of these systems [S-400 and Pantsir-S1] will further complicate the already difficult situation in the skies over Syria". From a Russian standpoint, however, such complications would affect the NATO and other aligned states operating over Syria whom now faced an air defence system of unprecedented capability. For the Russian part, the deployment reasoning was simple. If Russian aircraft were not to be protected by NATO and her allies honoring air incident avoidance protocol agreements or by adhering to international law regarding aircraft approaching or crossing international borders, then the Russian Federation would ensure the safety of those aircraft through direct military action.

In a twist of irony, just over one year after the 24 November 2015 air incident, Russia and Turkey began conducting joint military operations against forces in the North of Syria as both countries found common ground in opposing the policies and actions of the United States led coalition as Turkey drifted ever further apart from her NATO partners following a rift that had widened following a failed coup attempt in Turkey in summer 2016.

Page 119.120: Russian S-400 long range surface to air missile systems and Pantsir-S1 short range missile/gun air defence systems at Hmeymim air base in late 2015. MODRF

APPENDICES

Appendix I

Identified Su-24M's operating in Syria from September 2015-March 2016

White 04	
White 05	
While 25	
White 26	
White 27	
White 49	
White 71	
White 72	
White 74	
White 75	
White 76	
White 77	Returned to Russia on 16 March 2016
White 78	Returned to Russia on 16 March 2016
White 79	Returned to Russia on 16 March 2016
White 80	
White 81	Returned to Russia on 16 March 2016
White 83	Lost on 24 November 2015

GLOSSARY

ANS	Attack and Navigation System
APCT&TTC	Airborne Personnel Combat Training and Transition Training Centre
CCTC	Combat Conversion Training Centre
CWR	Collision Warning Radar
DoD	Department of Defence
ECM	Electronic Counter Measures
GPS	Global Positioning System
HQ	Headquarters
IFF	Identification Friend or Foe
IFV	Infantry Fighting Vehicle
Il	Ilyushin
INS	Inertial Navigation System
IR	Infrared
IRSTS	Infrared Search and Tracking System
ISIS	Islamic State of Iraq and the Levant (Also known as IS, ISIL and Daesh)
JSC	Joint Stock Company
kg	Kilogram
kg/cm^2	Kilogram/per centimetre squared
kgf	Kilogram force
kg/kgf/h	Kilogram/per kilogram force/per hour
kg/s	Kilograms per second
km	Kilometer
km/h	Kilometers per hour
KnAAPO	Komsomolsk-on-Amur Aircraft Production Association
l/m	Litres per minute
LTVSTS	Laser Television Search and Track System
m	meter
MFDS	Multi-Function Display Screen
MLRS	Multiple Launch Rocket System
mm	millimeter
MODRF	Ministry of Defence of the Russian Federation
NAPO	Novosibirsk Aircraft Plant, Chkalov
NATO	North Atlantic Treaty Organisation
NRS	Nose Radar System
OBS	On-Board Switchgear
OM	Objective Monitoring
POL	Petroleum Oli Lubricants
RWR	Radar Warning Receiver
SDA	Syrian Democratic Army
STOL	Short Take-Off and Landing

Su	Sukhoi
Tu	Tupolev
TV	Television
UAV	Uninhabited Air Vehicle
UHF	Ultra-High Frequency
US	United States
USSR	Union of Soviet Socialist Republics
V	Velocity
VHF	Very High Frequency
x	Times (multiplication)
±	Plus or minus
°	Degree(s)

ABOUT THE AUTHOR

Hugh, a historian and author with an extensive background in astro/geophysics and studies/research in the wider scientific, aeronautic, astronautic and nautical technical and historical fields, has published in excess of sixty books; non-fiction and fiction, writing under his given name as well as utilising several pseudonyms. He has also written for several international magazines, whilst his work has been used as reference for many other projects ranging from the aviation industry, international news corporations and film media to encyclopaedias, museum exhibits and the computer gaming industry. Hugh is a member of the institute of Physics, a member of the British Geophysics Association and is an elected Fellow of the Royal Astronomical Society. He currently resides in his native Scotland.

Other titles by the author include

Sukhoi T-50/PAK FA - Russia's 5th Generation 'Stealth' Fighter
Sukhoi Su-35S 'Flanker' E - Russia's 4++ Generation Super-Manoeuvrability Fighter
Sukhoi Su-34 'Fullback'
Sukhoi Su-30MKK/MK2/M2 - Russo Kitashiy Striker from Amur
MiG-35/D 'Fulcrum' F – Towards the Fifth Generation
Air War over Syria, Tu-160, Tu-95MS & Tu-22M3 - Cruise Missile and Bombing Strikes on Syria, November 2015-February 2016
Sukhoi Su-27SM(3)/SKM
Iskander - Mobile Tactical Aero-Ballistic/Cruise Missile Complex
Orbital/Fractional Orbit Bombardment System - The Soviet Globalnaya Raketa
Russian Non-Nuclear Attack Submarines – Project 877/877E/877EKM/Project 636/636.3 & Project 677/Amur 1650/950/S-1000
Russian/Soviet Aircraft Carrier & Carrier Aviation Design & Evolution Volume 1 - Seaplane Carriers, Project 71/72, Graf Zeppelin, Project 1123 ASW Cruiser & Project 1143-1143.4 Heavy Aircraft Carrying Cruiser
Light Battle Cruisers and the Second Battle of Heligoland Bight
British Battlecruisers of World War 1 - Operational Log, July 1914-June 1915
Eurofighter Typhoon - Storm over Europe
Tornado F.2/F.3 Air Defence Variant
Air to Air Missile Directory
North American F-108 Rapier - Mach 3 Interceptor
Convair YB-60 - Fort Worth Overcast
Boeing X-36 Tailless Agility Flight Research Aircraft
X-32 - The Boeing Joint Strike Fighter
X-35 - Progenitor to the F-35 Lightning II
X-45 Uninhabited Combat Air Vehicle
Into The Cauldron - The Lancaster MK.I Daylight Raid on Augsburg
Hurricane IIB Combat Log - 151 Wing RAF, North Russia 1941
RAF Meteor Jet Fighters in World War II, an Operational Log
Typhoon IA/B Combat Log - Operation Jubilee, August 1942
Defiant MK.I Combat Log - Fighter Command, May-September 1940
Blenheim MK.IF Combat Log - Fighter Command Day Fighter Sweeps/Night Interceptions, September 1939 - June 1940
Tomahawk I/II Combat Log - European Theatre, 1941-42
Fortress MK.I Combat Log - Bomber Command High Altitude Bombing Operations, July-September 1941
XF-92 - Convairs Arrow

www.ingramcontent.com/pod-product-compliance
Lightning Source LLC
Chambersburg PA
CBHW041527220426
43670CB00003B/51